University of Liverpool

Withdrawn from stock

12

21

Longman Geography Paperbacks

The Logic of Unity

Longman Geography Paperbacks

Editor: Professor R. W. Steel

Already published in this series

MIGRANTS AND MALARIA R. Mansell Prothero

COAL AND THE POWER INDUSTRIES IN POSTWAR BRITAIN E. S. Simpson

VIEWING WEATHER FROM SPACE E. C. Barrett

Geoffrey Parker

Extra-mural Tutor
University of Birmingham
Formerly Adult Education Tutor
South Shropshire

The Logic of Unity

An economic geography of the
Common Market

Longman

LONGMAN GROUP LIMITED
London

Associated companies, branches and representatives throughout the world

© Longman Group Ltd (formerly Longmans, Green and Co Ltd) 1968

First published 1968
Second impression 1970

SBN 582 31035 0

Printed in Great Britain by
T. & A. Constable Ltd., Edinburgh

To SAB

271795

'Les événements ne sont que l'écume des
choses; ce qui m'intéresse, c'est
la mer'

PAUL VALERY

Foreword

This series of geography paperbacks is concerned with practical and topical matters, and few subjects have given rise to more discussion in recent years than the problems and prospects of the Common Market in Europe and the nature of Britain's relationships with the countries of the European Economic Community.

The involvement of geographers with these problems has—for reasons suggested by the author in his preface—not been generally recognized, and Mr. Parker is the first to attempt such an appraisal, from a geographical viewpoint, of the significance of the economic union of the six Common Market countries of France, the German Federal Republic, Italy, Belgium, The Netherlands and Luxembourg. Such an account is of special importance because it is vital to appreciate the nature of the geographical background and to recognize the effects of the Common Market on the landscape, the economic development and the political allegiances of the European mainland.

No one is better equipped to write such a book than the author who through his work as an Adult Education Tutor in Shropshire is well aware of what people are thinking and of the types of questions on this topic that they are asking. With his great knowledge of the statistical and cartographic material available, he is able to throw light on many of the problems posed by the emergence of the Community, and readers of his book may well find themselves convinced, as I have been, of 'the logic of unity' as they study the case that he so cogently and logically presents.

R. W. STEEL
Department of Geography,
University of Liverpool
July 1968

Contents

Preface

It has been said that language is a way of concealing rather than revealing meaning, and the phrase 'common market' by which the progressive economic union of six European countries—France, West Germany, Italy, Belgium, the Netherlands and Luxembourg—has come to be known in many ways bears this out. The term conjures up the image of a monolithic sales organization, a sort of international supermarket, whose main business is making profits rather than trying to fulfil an internationalist ideal. This is in fact very far from the truth. The treaties establishing the European Communities—the correct title for the Common Market—had far-reaching intentions, and the 'founding fathers' included many convinced internationalists whose main aim was to rid Europe once and for all of national rivalry and the strife it creates. It is sad that so great and exciting a concept should have been saddled with the prosaic name of 'Common Market', but the term has now come into such general use that it must be accepted, however reluctantly, as a description of the organization.

The presence of this new grouping just across the Channel is now one of the established facts of life in Britain, and it has become a subject of considerable discussion and contention. Over the years since its foundation a vast amount has been written about it; most of this has concerned its political, economic, social and legal aspects, and the implications of these for Britain if and when this country becomes a member. The marketologists have their telescopes trained on Brussels much in the same way as astronomers watch the planets, and they record and interpret the events of the European cosmos with no doubt equal accuracy. However, so far there has been no book concerned with the geography of the organization, and this omission would appear to be due to two facts.

The first is that for the most part intelligent people in this country, and indeed in most others, appear to be still largely unaware that geography has far more to contribute to an understanding of current situations than the recitation of a few useful background facts. The discussion of world problems is generally considered to be the province of the economist, the sociologist, the political scientist or what you will, but geographers have not yet made very much impact in this sphere.

The second fact is that the geographical response to changes in political and economic conditions is a slow one. Treaties may be signed, tariffs lowered, freight rates and tax systems standardized, but it takes a long time for the effects of all this to be felt on the distribution of economic activities throughout the regions and countries to which they apply. When change has eventually come about, the establishment of cause and effect has often been difficult and sometimes even impossible.

At the present day both of these facts are in course of change. The study of applied geography is developing, and the merits of the geographical approach are coming to be realized by the practitioners of other disciplines and, in a more limited way, by the public at large. At the same time substantial changes have become perceptible in the principal features of the economic geography of the six countries, and many of these are clearly related to the politico-economic developments associated with the Common Market.

It is the object of this book to present a picture of the distribution of economic activity in the Common Market as a whole, and to study the changes which have occurred since the organization came into being. It considers the extent to which these changes are related to the establishment of the Common Market, and the significance of other factors which might in any case have been operative. These distributional changes are considered not merely as the aftermath of the others, but as themselves an essential prerequisite to the successful establishment of the new unit as a viable and permanent feature of the world's economic and political organization.

This book is intended for all who have an interest in the absorbing and important subject of the Common Market, and wish to look at the whole question from a new angle. Those studying economic geography courses will find that the book treats this large part of Western Europe as a whole, ignoring the national frontiers which have been for so long the basic boundaries in conventional regional analysis. Students of economics and international organizations may find some enlightenment in an approach which is probably new to them.

I must acknowledge my indebtedness to the writers of the various books and publications that are specified in the reference section at the end. I also acknowledge with gratitude the help afforded by the London Embassies of each of the six countries, and that of the United States of America. My especial thanks go to the staff of the London Office of the Information Service of the European Communities who have unfailingly supplied me with up-to-date statistical and other material as it has appeared.

Professor R. W. Steel, the editor of this series, has always been available to give advice, and his constant encouragement has made my task of writing far easier. The maps were admirably drawn from my roughs by Mr. Alan G. Hodgkiss of the Department of Geography, University of Liverpool.

Finally, a special word of thanks is due to my wife for her valuable comments and criticisms, and for preparing the manuscript and the index.

Geoffrey Parker

Shrewsbury, July 1968

List of Tables

List of Maps and Graphs

1 The Whole and the Parts

A glance at the globe, or a map of the world, will show that the continent of Europe is no more than a small peninsula jutting out from the western side of Asia. But its importance has been out of all proportion to its small size, since it was in Europe that modern technical civilization first came into being, and, from the seventeenth century to well on into the twentieth, made the continent the principal seat of world power. This power was consolidated politically in the global empires which the Europeans carved for themselves out of every continent.

The map will also show that Europe is a political patchwork quilt made up of nations ranging in size from small to minute, but none, by world standards, large. Throughout the centuries this pattern has been constantly modified as new nations have sprung up and old ones declined, but in the west of the continent it has not now been altered substantially for a hundred years. In fact it is a truer representation of political realities in the late nineteenth than in the mid-twentieth century, and this is largely attributable to the transformation of Europe's situation, both internally and externally, since the Second World War. The patchwork appears to indicate that this small part of the globe is still run by fifteen or so local authorities, each in absolute control of its own strip of territory and concerned as in the past only with promoting its own interests. This is a false picture since the political map does not reveal the extent to which interdependence has become a reality, one of the foremost expressions of which is the European Economic Community.

The Community was founded in 1951, the member states being the Federal German Republic (generally known as West Germany), France, Italy, the Netherlands, Belgium, and Luxembourg. At its most far reaching this organization is an attempt to establish one nation instead of six, and the first stage in this is the progressive economic merger which has been in process since 1951. The replacement of nationalism by internationalism is no new ideal in this part of the world. The Roman Empire succeeded in unifying practically the whole of Western Europe, and four hundred years later the territory controlled by Charlemagne was remarkably similar to that occupied by the Community some 1,150 years later. Since the breaking up of Charlemagne's empire, many efforts have been made to re-establish unity, and in most cases these have been attempts by one or other of the individual countries to impose its will on the others. At various times England, Spain, France and Germany have all striven for supremacy with greater or less success, but never was an individual nation's power great enough to achieve permanent domination over all the others.

The Community differs from these past attempts in many ways, and perhaps most radically because it seeks to establish unity by agreement. It is also different because it has not been heralded by fanfares of trumpets and spectacular political gymnastics, but is using the quieter road of progressive economic integration. This integration is now steadily eroding away the individual foundations of the participating states, and doing it, strangely enough, with their own support.

The process has been aided by three things which have made the idea of unity a very attractive one at the present day. These are the weakness of the individual countries, the great possibilities which cooperation and combination now appear to offer, and the increased feasibility of union in modern economic and technical conditions.

In 1945 continental Western Europe was devastated and its industries had been brought virtually to a standstill. Years of concentration on armaments followed by the havoc of total war had dislocated the economies of all but the few neutrals. By 1948, three years after the end of the war, the steel output of the whole area was still only 25·8 million tons, as compared with 35·1 million in 1938.* Likewise coal output was 196·5 million tons compared with 250·5 in the former year. The two most powerful countries and the two great rivals of the past century, France and Germany, were so weakened that the most sensible way to bring about recovery seemed to be through cooperation. This was started in 1948 with the establishment of the Organization for European Economic Cooperation (OEEC)

---

* These figures are for the OECD countries, excluding the United Kingdom and Yugoslavia.

which channelled massive United States aid to Europe, and so began
the slow process of general recovery.

In addition to the effects of the war, it was also apparent that the
nations of Western Europe had now come to possess a number of
built-in weaknesses. Throughout the later nineteenth and early
twentieth centuries these nations had become more and more inward-looking with carefully controlled external affairs and trading
relations, and their frontiers had grown into high walls of tariffs,
quotas, and restrictions on the movement of capital and labour.
After the rapid increase in industrial production which characterized
the late nineteenth century, it had come to be believed that European consumption was now saturated and that new consumers had
to be found in order to avoid total collapse. Each nation turned
naturally to its overseas empire for salvation, and the bonds were
drawn ever tighter as empire came to be regarded as a vehicle for
giving the nation a new lease of life.

Although in many cases the economic significance of colonies was
exaggerated, they indubitably possessed a psychological value which
considerably influenced national policies. Besides suggesting a way
out of difficulties they increased the national self-esteem and encouraged the imperial neighbours in their European semi-detacheds
to 'go it alone' and cut their mutual contacts to a minimum.

Nationalist movements in the colonies put paid to this state of
affairs, and after 1945 there was a steady flow of former possessions
to independence. At the end of the Second World War the countries
which were later to join the Community had been the centres of
global empires covering 7,113,200 sq. km, nearly seven times their
own combined area, while twenty years later only 303,000 sq. km
was left under their control. The loss of the colonies did not have the
catastrophic economic effects which jingos and Jeremiahs had often
predicted, but the idea of salvation through imperialism thereby
ceased to be a practical proposition, and other solutions to the problems of national self-insufficiency had to be canvassed.

The third element in the weakness of the European nations was
their relative loss of importance in face of developments in other
parts of the world. The most important of such developments was the
rise of the super-powers, the United States of America and the
Soviet Union, which by 1945 had become in all ways the most
powerful countries in the world. Their core regions, the north-east of
the United States and the centre of European Russia, are contiguous
with great continental interiors, and huge areas of these had been
incorporated and to a large degree assimilated into the national

3

territories. Thus they successfully accomplished what the European imperialists had unsuccessfully attempted, so creating nations of vast proportions. In 1945 the USSR was the largest nation on earth and had an area of 22·4 million sq. km, nine times that of the whole of Western Europe and forty times that of its largest country, France. Her population was as great as that of the United Kingdom, West Germany, France, and Italy combined.

The production of the super-powers was also commensurate with their great size. By 1952, the year ECSC came into operation, France's steel production of 10·9 million tons was one-third that of the USSR and one-eighth that of the USA. Italy's production of 3·5 million tons was one-eleventh that of the USSR and one-twenty-fifth that of the USA (Table 1). That this decline was to a large extent relative can be seen from the fact that in 1952 the West German steel output of 18·7 million tons was actually more than had been produced by the whole of Germany in 1913 (17 million tons). The essential difference was that while in 1913 Germany produced 20 per cent of the world's steel, in 1952 West Germany's greater output was only 8·7 per cent of it. It has been estimated that in 1900 Western Europe accounted for some nine-tenths of the world's industrial output, while by the early 1950s it was producing only three-quarters that of the United States alone.

Unity aims not only at countering national weakness, but also at bringing more positive advantages. It is obvious that a large economic unit must be more powerful than its small constituents, but it is also true that its economic efficiency can be far greater than just the sum of the parts. It creates an economic environment conducive to large scale production, industrial concentration, and the movement without hindrance of capital, labour, raw materials, and goods. Specializations can take place in those localities most favourable to them, and resources can be used in the most productive manner without artificial restrictions. In envisaging all this the European statesmen had their eyes firmly fixed on the great 'common market' of the United States. As Paul Spaak put it, 'There is no manufacturing firm in Europe which is big enough to take advantage of the most powerful American machinery', and the same could be said with equal truth of practically every aspect of industrial activity.

The European nations had thus become in many ways impediments to a full exploitation of the continent's potential. 'What is being integrated,' said Walter Hallstein in 1961, 'is the part played by the nation states in creating the conditions within which economic

4

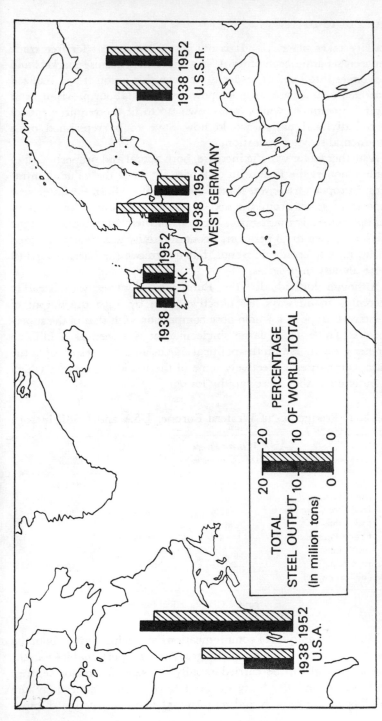

Fig. 1. Crude steel output of the four major producers—USA, USSR, Western Germany and United Kingdom, 1938 and 1952.

1938 1952
U.S.S.R.

1938 1952
WEST GERMANY

1952

1938
U.K.

PERCENTAGE
OF WORLD TOTAL

20   20
10   10
0   0

TOTAL
STEEL OUTPUT
(In million tons)

1938 1952
U.S.A.

5

activity takes place. .... It is not just a movement for free trade between separate economies. It is a movement to fuse markets and economies into one.' In order to achieve this fusion it was realized that such features as transport, power supply, labour provision, and capital investment which had grown up to fit the requirements of each individual nation would now have to be replanned on a continental scale of operation.

A further factor was the increase, both actual and proportional, in trade amongst the European countries. By 1952 the value of intra-West European trade was three times that of 1938. In the latter year exports of goods from the six Community countries to Western Europe generally made up 51 per cent of their total, while by 1952 this had grown to 58 per cent. Economic unity was clearly designed not to initiate economic trends, but to remove the barriers against those already in progress.

Although individually the European countries were steadily becoming in all ways less effective, even by 1952 the output of Western Europe as a whole bore comparison with that of the super-powers (Table 1). A large single market was seen as a fillip to further growth, and on the political side as an aid to restoring to the European nations collectively some of the world importance which as individuals they were rapidly losing.

Table 1. Production of Western Europe, USA and USSR in 1952

	Western Europe (OECD countries)	USA	USSR
Hard Coal (mill. tons)	954·9	457·6	215·0
Iron Ore Concentrate (mill. tons)	37·4	50·0	30·5
Crude Petroleum (mill. tons)	5·7	309·5	47·0
Electricity (billion kw hr)	291·3	465·3	119·0

(Source: OECD Statistical Survey)

Modern techniques of communication have helped bring about the consolidation of all these advantages. Air transport enables passengers and freight to be carried rapidly between the major centres, while speed and flexibility on land have been enhanced by the building of trunk roads and motorways. The construction of pipelines and electricity transmission lines has made possible the movement of power and power-producing materials over long distances, and the improvement of ports and interior waterways has expedited and cheapened the transport of heavy goods. Radio, television, and long distance telephone have made the transmission of news and information virtually instantaneous, and have helped make the continent and its peoples familiar to one another as never before. Perhaps an even more profound result has been achieved by the millions of tourists who each year familiarize themselves with one another's environments, and by taking home new ideas contribute to increasing the similarities in many aspects of life from one end of Europe to the other.

Yet in spite of this coincidence of favourable factors there was never a possibility after the Second World War of the unification of all the European countries. The states of Eastern Europe were soon brought together by communist ideology and associated themselves closely in almost every way with the Soviet Union. There were thus left the sixteen countries of non-communist Europe, most of which were represented on the Council of Europe when it first met in 1949. However, two years later only six of these chose to embark on the first stages of economic union by setting up the European Coal and Steel Community (See Appendix). The reasons why this should have been so are firmly rooted in the continent's geography.

The territory of Western Europe has an area of nearly three million sq. km. Geographically it consists of a trunk from which four prongs or extensions diverge (Fig. 2). In outline trunk Europe is a tilted quadrilateral bounded on the north by the North Sea-Channel coasts, on the west by the Bay of Biscay, on the south by the Alps and Pyrenees, and on the east by the dividing line between the two Germanies. The area enclosed in this way is a little over 900,000 sq. km, and is occupied roughly by the territories of France, West Germany, the Benelux countries and Switzerland. Of the four extensions, those to the south—Iberia and Italy—are peninsulas separated from the core by high mountains, while those to the north —the British Isles and Scandinavia—are almost entirely insular in relation to it except for Jutland which is attached at Schleswig.

The physical character of the trunk is the result of its position at the western end of the series of parallel relief features which extend from east to west across Europe. Here they form three belts which transcend national frontiers and produce three large-scale or macroregions these being the northern plain, the central uplands and the southern mountains (Fig. 3). The plain is low-lying, and only rarely reaches 300 metres in height. It is flattest around the composite delta of the Rhine in the Netherlands and northern Belgium, and most

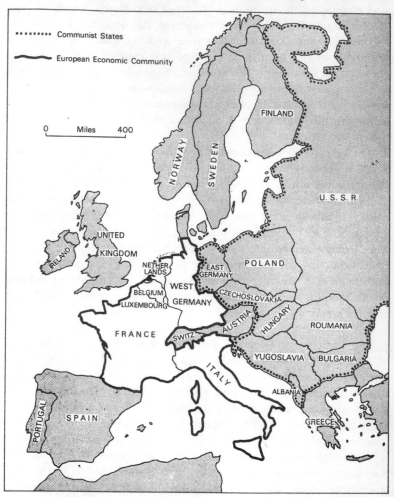

Fig. 2. The European Economic Community.

hilly in the Paris Basin and western France where rock folding followed by weathering have produced the well-known scarp dip formations. The plain extends southward into the neighbouring uplands in a number of embayments, the most notable of these being the Aquitaine and Paris Basins in France and the Cologne and Münster Bays in Germany.

8

The central uplands by contrast form a highly complex region which swings around from the Böhmerwald in the east to the Massif Central in the west. It consists for the most part of high

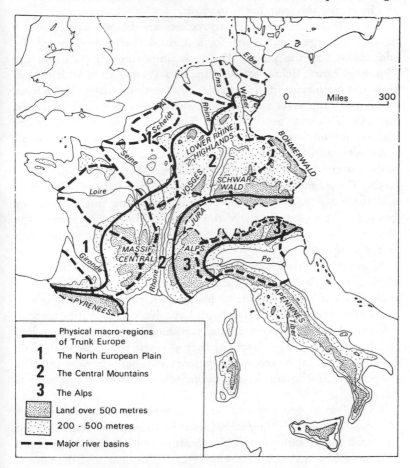

Fig. 3. The physical regions of the Community.

plateaux in places capped by rugged peaks and surrounded by deep valleys. The landscape is most complex and intricate in southern Germany, and here plateau heights vary between 1,000 and 1,500 metres. In the French Massif Central features are rather simpler and the land higher, reaching over 2,000 metres in places. To the south of these uplands are the Alps and the Pyrenees which have a generally east-west alignment, although the Alps swing southward in the region of the Franco-Italian border to reach the coast in the Ligurian

Sea. The mountains are bare and rugged with heights averaging 3,000 to 4,500 metres, and they are separated by deep valleys, some of which follow the geology from east to west while others, mainly cut by rivers, run from north to south.

These three dissimilar macro-regions are bound together by a number of large rivers which form natural routeways between the mountains and the plains. The most important of them are the Garonne, Loire, Seine, Rhine, Ems and Weser, all of which drain from the mountains to the northern and western coasts. The Rhône is the only large river flowing southward following the gap between the Massif Central and the Alps. This gap is the most important line of communication between north-west Europe and the Mediterranean, and the valleys of the Garonne and the Seine link up with it over the Carcassonne Gap and the Morvan plateau respectively. The Rhine valley connects with the Rhône at the Belfort gap, and there are many passes over the Alps leading to the Po valley beyond. The most easterly of the major north-flowing rivers—the Weser—is backed by mountains which form a barrier to the lands to the south of it.

Since these great valleys and their tributaries are the most obvious routes by land and water, the coincidence along them of the major lines of internal transport has given them considerable economic importance. The riparian lands have evolved in mutual association and dependence, created and sustained by ease of contact, and this has helped to bind them together as single economic units. The bond is closest in the mountains where the relief otherwise impedes movement, and loosest in the plains where there are few natural barriers.

Looked at in geographical terms, it was the countries of trunk Europe together with Italy but without Switzerland which combined to found the Community. Their centuries-old political separation had its origins in the physical character of this area, and the same is now true of their reason for wishing to come together.

France, the largest of them, takes up nearly a half the Community's area, but has not much more than a quarter of its population (Table 2). It first became a separate political unit with the break-up of the empire of Charlemagne in the ninth century, and at the end of the feudal period the Paris basin became the cradle of the new French state. This area was agriculturally rich and easily controlled, and it became the base from which the local princes—later the French kings—brought the whole of the country under their political influence. Expansion into the poorer and not readily defensible territories to the west and south presented few problems, and by the fifteenth century the French state already stretched to the Atlantic and the Mediterranean. To the east expansion was far more difficult, and it was the French urge to find 'natural frontiers' in this direction which was one of the main causes of the great European wars of the seventeenth and eighteenth centuries. The answer to the unsatisfactory frontiers in this direction was seen by Louis XIV as expansion to the Rhine, but a European coalition, led by England and the Netherlands ensured that this did not occur, and the only relic of the drive to the Rhine is now the German-speaking province of Alsace

Table 2. Area, Population and Density per sq. km of the Community countries, 1966

Country	Area ('000 sq. km)	Population ('000)	Density (per sq. km)
Germany (FR)	248·5	59,638	240
France	551·2	49,440	90
Italy	301·2	51,859	172
Netherlands	33·5	12,455	372
Belgium	30·5	9,523	312
Luxembourg	2·6	335	129
Community	1,167·5	183,250	157

(Source: Basic Statistics of the Community 1967. Statistical Office of the European Community)

It has been the policy of the French state to carry out a high degree of centralization based on Paris, and this is clearly seen in the pattern of the road and rail systems. During the present century there has also been considerable industrial concentration on Paris, and this has now made it into the economic as well as the political heart of the country. One French geographer, J. L. Gravier, has talked of 'Paris dans le désert français', and there is indeed an extreme example here of that elephantiasis of the capital and its region which is to a certain extent a feature of most industrial countries.

Until the early nineteenth century France was without question the most powerful state in the whole of Europe, but with the coming of the Industrial Revolution, the inadequate and inconvenient supplies of coal, and at first of suitable iron ore, put her at a considerable disadvantage, and she began to lose ground to those countries, notably Germany and Britain, which possessed large resources of them both. However, with the changes in geographical values brought about by new types of manufacture and new sources of energy, she has now had a considerable revival, although overall output remains well behind that of West Germany.

Ever since the rapid industrialization of Germany in the last quarter of the nineteenth century, which she herself found it impossible to match, France has developed a great fear of German power. Many Frenchmen have seen this enshrined in the great Ruhr coal/steel complex, and it was argued that, if this could somehow be taken away from Germany, the danger would be eliminated. After 1918 this idea was approached in many ways ranging from the detachment of the Rhine territories from the Reich to outright occupation, and to many people the Coal and Steel Community of 1952 was a continuation of this policy in a milder form. The idea of the Community as a 'cage for the German tiger' began to change, however, as France realized the very real positive advantages that could accrue to her out of economic unity with her neighbours, and, as her African territories gained their independence, she became more willing to turn to the Community as a source of future strength.

Although having an area less than half that of France, West Germany's population is by far the larger of the two (Table 2). Like France, almost its entire area was within Charlemagne's empire, but unlike the former it did not solidify into a nation state. Most of the west bank of the Rhine became in the ninth century part of Lotharingia, the middle kingdom, which stretched from the Low Countries southward into northern Italy, but this narrow territory was quite unviable and remained a bone of contention to our own day. Right up to the late nineteenth century most of the Rhinelands remained politically fragmented, and it was not until 1871 that the German parts became united, and then it was under the leadership of Prussia.

In these circumstances a West German core area is a rather nebulous concept, but the middle Rhine from Cologne to Frankfurt has had all the makings of one. The all-German Diet normally met in one or other of its towns, and before unity Frankfurt was the only city which approached the rôle of a metropolis for the whole region. With the establishment of the German Empire, and the movement of the centre of power eastward to Berlin, the political importance of the area declined, but the setting up of the Federal Republic in 1954 with its capital at Bonn brought importance back again and gave to the old core region a definite political function which it had lacked in the past. If we stretch the area northward to include the Ruhr, we have here also the economic core region which has been the major seat of German industrial power for a hundred years (Fig. 4).

The Federal Republic is made up of two very dissimilar areas, the plain to the north and the mountains to the south, and both of them

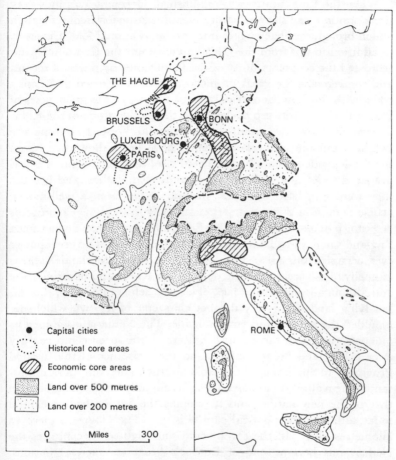

Fig. 4. Core areas and capitals.

are sections through the macro-regions stretching across Europe from east to west. Physically the country is a slice cut through them from the Alps to the North Sea, with hardly any well-defined frontiers to west or east, and this has made it very vulnerable to attack. The great link between the mountains and the plains is the Rhine basin, but both the source and the mouth of the great river are outside German territory. German expansionism during the first half of the present century can be seen as a response to these conditions, and as an attempt to bring the whole of the Rhinelands into the nation's economic orbit, just as France had tried and failed to do in previous centuries.

When the Community was established, Germany was in a very weak position, and she was naturally enthusiastic for an organization which brought her back again into the international fold. However, in addition to this from the German viewpoint the Community has recreated the economic unity of the Rhinelands by peaceful means, and so overcome the great problems which had existed to German trade with the Low Countries, and to the use of the great ports of Rotterdam and Antwerp to deal with the foreign trade of the Ruhr.

Between these two giants of continental Western Europe are Belgium and the Netherlands which have been allowed to retain their independence both because neither of their big neighbours was prepared to let them fall into the hands of the other, and because they were supported by Great Britain. It has been a well-known article of faith in this country that an army in the Low Countries is 'a pistol pointed at the heart of England', and it has always been England's policy in alliance with others to ensure that no great power ever occupied this area. The territory of the Netherlands consists basically of the great multiple delta of the Rhine and its tributaries, and although it has a total lack of clearly defined frontiers, this flat low-lying land has a very distinct character of its own which has moulded the nature of its economic life. The Netherlands gained its independence from the Spanish Empire in the seventeenth century after a long and bitter conflict, and the resistance of the 'United Provinces' to Spain was led by Holland, the richest and most important of them all. With independence, its capital, Amsterdam, became that of the new nation, and it remains the administrative capital today although the political capital is now The Hague, a mere 45 kilometres away. In the seventeenth and eighteenth centuries the Netherlands became one of Europe's great commercial nations, helped by her rich agriculture, fine ports, and strategic position. The country's prosperity centred on the province of Holland, which developed into the economic as well as the political core region. Today this has become even more emphasized and has crystallized into that group of great cities known as the Randstad, which includes Rotterdam, the Hague, Amsterdam, and Utrecht.

While the Netherlands has in all ways a very high degree of homogeneity, Belgium consists of two parts which are physically very different from one another. The country is in many ways a microcosm of West Germany, with the great plain in the north and the Ardennes mountains in the south, while the mouth of the great Sambre-Meuse routeway is, like the Rhine in Germany, out of the country's direct political control. In the north are the Flemings, a Catholic people akin to the Dutch, and in the south are the Walloons who are French and Protestant. The differences between the two were accentuated in the last century by the industrialization and growing prosperity of the south which led to growing Flemish resentment. When the country became independent in 1839 Brussels was chosen as the capital because it is central both geographically and linguistically, and it rapidly grew to become one of the largest cities in Western Europe. The area with the most historical associations of a national character is Flanders, but industrialization is now very widespread, and one can tentatively pick out an economic core which centres on the Brussels-Antwerp axis.

European unity is more important to both these small states than it is to either of their great neighbours. Not only is their security dependent on the preservation of peace in Western Europe, but their commercial relations with the other countries are on a very large scale. Being at the mouth of the Rhine routeway, they are the natural entrepôts for a large area of the continent stretching from the North Sea to Switzerland. This is reflected in their foreign trade which was in 1952 worth about one-third of the national product in each case, the highest proportion in any European countries, and nearly a half of this trade was with the other countries of the Community.

Luxembourg, one of the world's smallest states, with an area of only 2,600 sq. km, is a Germanic dialect speaking part of the Moselle basin which, after being incorporated in the German customs union in 1871, decided to become independent in 1918. However, the independence of so small a state can be only nominal in modern conditions, and as early as 1923 it joined Belgium to form the BLEU (Belgium-Luxembourg Economic Union) which has single tariffs and currency.

Italy, the third large country in the Community, has an area slightly greater than that of West Germany, and its population is a little more than that of France. It is the sole Community country which is not a part of trunk Europe, and it is separated from it by the Alpine mountains, which, although a great natural divide, have not been such a barrier to contacts with the trunk as have, for example, the Pyrenees and the English Channel. This is partly because Italy has never controlled the main mass of the mountains and so could never effectively stem incursions from the north. In addition to this, unlike England and Spain which had both achieved a high degree of national unity by the fifteenth century, it was until a hundred years ago merely a collection of small independent states. On and off most of these had been under foreign domination, and it was this which made Metternich refer contemptuously to the peninsula as 'a geographical expression'.

The girdle of mountains around the north of the country is the greatest physical barrier in the whole Community, and the mountainous nature of the peninsula itself has meant that it was difficult to find an area from which political control could be effectively exercised. The Po basin could have performed this function, but it was handicapped by persistent foreign interference from across the Alps and by the fact that Rome remained the focus of the national aspirations. With the achievement of unity, Rome became the capital but the north, and particularly the upper Po region, was confirmed as the economic heart, and as it developed it tended more and more to impoverish the economic life of other parts of the country. However, as a whole Italy remained economically very weak until after the Second World War, due largely to its great lack of coal and the other raw materials of industry. In recent years, however, economic changes affecting the whole of Europe, together with the discovery of new resources have been altering the situation, and she has now joined France and Germany as one of the great industrial nations of the world.

Italy's decision to join the Community can be related both to her traditionally close ties with the countries of trunk Europe and also to a number of other circumstances. Due mainly to her paucity of raw materials, power, and capital investment, she was a poor and relatively weak country, and it was felt that she would benefit from membership because this would open large and affluent markets to her industries and encourage the inflow of capital. On the political side, it had come to be realized that the policy of expansion pursued between the wars had been a failure and that now amalgamation with a greater Europe was a more realistic course.

We will now go on to look at the main features of the economy of the Community from the geographical point of view, and attempt to assess the extent to which its existence has decreased the importance of the national patterns of activity and replaced them with new supra-national ones.

2 The New Mobility

The relative efficiency of all economic activity is dependent upon the ease with which raw materials, manufactured goods, and people can be moved from place to place, and in modern industrial societies this need is catered for by roads, railways, ships, and other specialized forms of transport. The coming of the Community together with the changes which are accompanying it have necessitated radical adjustments to the transport systems of the six countries without which such changes would at best be very imperfectly achieved.

These adjustments are taking place in two complementary ways: there are the applications of technical advance to a diversification of the methods of transport, and there are the politico-economic changes brought about by the existence of the Community which have increased the scale on which transport operations must be planned. It is axiomatic that economic integration cannot be brought about without a common transport policy, and it is therefore the Community's intention to standardize freight rates, to introduce unfettered competition among the various sectors, and, what is of greatest importance, to weld together the separate national systems so as to provide a network adapted to serve the needs of the Community as a whole.

The Treaty of Rome makes no specific provision for Community action in altering the transport pattern to fit the new conditions, but the first memorandum on the proposed common transport policy published in 1961 said that the Community had a part to play in 'establishing a transport system in which the development of infrastructures would be harmonized so as to meet the needs of the Common Market'. The coordination of transport is therefore considered as being an essential accompaniment to economic policy generally, and since 1959 a series of inter-governmental conferences have tried to agree on the means for achieving this.[1] In February

1966 a system of consultation among the six countries was instituted which obliges member governments to consult with the others before they put into effect investment plans of general Community interest involving the development of communication links and the expansion of existing ones. This has already produced notable results, particularly in the planning of motorways across frontiers, and the Community is acting as a clearing house for these various plans, while making a positive contribution through the loans being given for selected projects by the European Investment Bank.

The magnitude of the Community's task has been increased by the fact that each country's transport system has been built up to meet its own particular needs in the light of its physical, economic and strategic circumstances, and each is unique in its emphasis, its methods of operation and in the features of its geographical pattern. In France transport has been regarded first and foremost as a public service under close state scrutiny and control, and is based upon the railways which carry more freight than do the country's roads and waterways combined. Economic operation has been secondary to what are considered as being the national interests as a whole, so there have been few closures and the network remains very comprehensive with practically every canton having its own station. Competition from road carriers is restricted by licensing, and the navigable waterways have, with certain outstanding exceptions, not been able to compete very effectively.

Geographically the most outstanding feature of the French transport system is the concentration of roads and railway lines from all parts of the country on Paris, and, with certain important exceptions, the lack of effective inter-provincial connections. In most cases it is not so much that there are no provincial routes as that, because of the centripetal growth of the French economy, they have been used far less than the lines which radiate from the capital. Thus the Gironde-Rhône routeway through the Carcassonne gap takes road, rail and canal, but the latter, the Canal du Midi, is very small by modern standards. The greater part of bulk freight carriage is in the north-east of the country, and it is only here that water transport is used considerably. The main interior waterways are the Seine as far as Paris, the Oise-St Quentin canal which connects the capital with the Nord industrial region, and (of course) the French stretch of the Rhine which, together with its tributaries, gives the east of the country access to the Community's greatest inland waterway system.

German transport policy has been called the extreme case of state interference, and in the past this has had a great deal of truth. It is

seen in the most individual feature of the German system, the autobahns, which were begun in the early 1930s and have since been
continually extended. Originally constructed largely for social and
strategic reasons, they have since become of great economic importance and were the prototype for the motorways built later by other
European nations. In spite of this, the railways still carry the largest
quantity of freight, while road and water share the remainder almost
equally.

The geography of German transport is totally different from that
of France. The railway network was already complete in its essentials
by the time of unification in 1871, and it is based as much upon
provincial and state capitals such as Cologne, Frankfurt, Stuttgart,
and Munich as it is upon Berlin. In contrast to this the autobahns
were built in and for a unified Germany, and they link together the
great industrial regions of the west and connect them with Berlin.
After the division of the country in 1945, economic activity between
the zones was very small, and those autobahns converging on Berlin
from the west were left with the essentially political function of
sustaining the western enclave but became of much diminished
economic importance. The country's waterways are absolutely
dominated by the Rhine and its navigable tributaries which together
carry the overwhelming part of the water-borne traffic and which
exert a considerable influence throughout the whole of the north-east
of the Community.

Table 3. Length of the Community Transport Systems 1966

Country	Length of Rail Line Operated (km)	Length of Inland Waterways in Use (km)	Length of Motorways (km)	Length of Oil Pipelines (km)
Germany (FR)	30,434	4,424	3,372	1,014
France	37,850	7,561	854	1,542
Italy	15,979	2,354	1,705	1,451
Netherlands	3,232	6,044	707	456
Belgium	4,441	1,535	318	—
Luxembourg	338	37	—	—
Community	92,274	21,965	6,956	4,463

(Sources: Statistical Office of the European Communities and national information services)

The German communications pattern is based upon two routeways, one from north to south and the other from east to west. The
former joins together the great industrial areas along the Rhine and

the latter connects Berlin with the western industrial regions by the Elbe, the Mittelland canal and the autobahns. The division of the country has resulted in a weakening of the east-west axis and a strengthening of the north-south one, which is now by far the more important for the internal movement of goods.

While in Germany each of the three major forms of interior transport has a large share of total traffic, in Italy three-quarters is carried by the roads and practically all the remainder by rail. Until quite recently, however, the railways were the major form of transport and the road system was very poor. Italy's economic advancement has been handicapped by many things, none more serious than the inadequacy of the transport system and the physical obstacles in the way of improving it. The basic problems are the country's great length of over 1,000 km from north to south, and the difficulty of east-west communication across the Apennines. Until the 1930s there were no through rail services from the north to the south and the roads were in a very poor state. The main Italian answer to this problem has been to build a comprehensive system of motorways, and by 1966 1,700 km had been finished and a further 3,000 km are due for completion by 1970. The most spectacular one is the Autostrada del Sole with a length of 755 km from Milan to Naples; it crosses the Apennines between Bologna and Florence and then follows the Arno and Tiber valleys.[2] These and similar projects have contributed to making the roads overwhelmingly the most important form of freight transport in Italy. Interior waterways make very little contribution largely owing to the nature of the land surface and the rainfall regime, and only the Po and its tributaries are of any importance whatsoever. The difficulties of internal communication have, however, made coastal shipping of considerable importance, and the total volume of freight carried in this way is about one-third that of the railways. The main arteries of the peninsula extend along the western and eastern coasts and there are still few major transverse links, but the upper Po is a hub from which lines radiate over the Alps to northern Europe, across the Apennines to Genoa and down the valley to Venice and the Adriatic.

In the Netherlands the interior waterways play an even more overwhelming part in the carriage of freight than do the roads in Italy, and in 1966 86 per cent of all the goods handled went by water. The country has 6,044 km of waterways, 2,200 of these being navigable to vessels of over 1,000 tons, and every Dutch province can be reached by them. This concentration on water transport is the most remarkable feature of the Dutch system, and is due to the physical nature of the country which is part of the great composite delta of the Rhine, and to the country's entrepôt function at the mouth of the Community's most important route into the interior. The largest tonnages are carried by the Waal, Lek, and Nieuwe Waterweg from Rotterdam to the coast, the North Sea Canal from Ijmuiden to Amsterdam and the Amsterdam-Rhine Canal.

It is the Netherlands' transport policy to foster competition among the three methods so as to provide the user with the best available service. As a result the rail system has been allowed to contract to just over 3,000 km, and the 'Netherlands tramways' as they have been called now cover the country with fast and frequent services and are the only railways in the Community which are paying their way. Their main importance is for passenger travel, and the 27 million tons of freight which they carried in 1966 made up only between one and two per cent of that moved in the country. As the share of the railways has decreased, so that of the roads has gone up, and the country already had over 700 km of motorway in 1966 with a lot more being planned.

Although Belgium is so near to the Netherlands, and the two are closely associated economically, their communications systems have little in common either in their characteristics or their running methods. In no other Community country is there such a balance as exists in Belgium between rail, road and water carriers, and it is the aim of the government to coordinate their efforts. The northern part of the country is best served, and here are found all the interior waterways, motorways, and most of the electrified railways. The focus of the roads and railways is the Brussels-Antwerp area which in many ways resembles the Paris-Le Havre axis in France, but the dominant orientation of the major routes is from the coast eastward following the natural line of movement into the Rhinelands.

Luxembourg's transport system has been geared primarily to the needs of the iron and steel industry, and these have in the past been catered for almost entirely by the railways. They are administered by a board of French, Belgian, and Luxembourg directors and are closely integrated into the systems of their greater neighbours. The most important freight carrying lines are those westward into Belgium and southward to Lorraine. Although very centrally situated in the Community, Luxembourg is not one of its main centres of gravity, and there are fears that the Duchy may be by-passed by the 'Euroroutes' and so become 'a branch line on a continental scale'.

Besides these differences in the nature of the transport arrangements in each country, economic nationalism is most forcefully expressed in each country's desire for independent access to the sea, and for lines of internal communication which do not use the territory of neighbouring countries and so depend upon their goodwill. An example of this is the Dunkirk-Strasbourg railway, from the coast through the Nord coalfield to Lorraine taking a route which is entirely on French soil. Connecting together as it does the country's principal heavy industrial regions, it is one of the most important freight-carrying lines, but takes few through passengers.

Although the Rhine has been an international waterway since the early nineteenth century and traffic on it controlled by international conventions, it has still suffered political disadvantages in the eyes of the riparian states which have consequently attempted to obviate their dependence upon it. The Germans built the port of Emden adjacent to the Dutch frontier and linked it with the Ruhr by the Dortmund-Ems canal, completed in 1904 as an all-German feeder from the North Sea to the Middle Rhinelands. Similarly the construction of the Canal Juliana in the Netherlands, the Albert canal in Belgium and the Grand Canal d'Alsace were all motivated more by national than by economic considerations.[3]

The task of fusing these six—or at least five—very individual transport systems is not an easy one, but it is made easier by the fact that many new methods of transport have grown up almost entirely in the conditions of the Community and so have been adapted from the start to a continental rather than a national scale of operations. Even with existing methods much-needed modernization is being carried out with the needs of the Community as a whole in mind. It has been said rather unkindly that the age of the Community's railroad equipment often rivals that of cognac of the best quality, and, indeed, the system which was inherited in the early 1950s had not much altered geographically or technically for many years. Considerable capital has now been invested in improvements, notably doubling and electrification of the track, and priority has been given to a number of international lines, notably the Paris-Cologne, Paris-Metz-Mannheim, and the St Gotthard and Brenner routes across the Alps. In 1963 a loan of 24 million dollars was obtained from the European Investment Bank for the electrification of the Chambéry-Modane-Genoa line through the Graian Alps, thus connecting the north Italian industrial region with the Rhône Corridor. The lines from the Low Countries to the Ruhr which in the past because of political factors have been of less importance than might have been expected have now been electrified and integrated with the German system.

As we have already seen, national policies on the rôle to be played by the railways vary considerably, but it is the intention of the Commission that subsidies of any sort must be brought to an end and all railway systems made economically viable by 1972.

While the transformation of the railways is basically the adaptation of a system which evolved in quite different economic and political conditions, the motorways are a new form of transport, and except for Germany's, they have virtually all been built since the Second World War. In 1952 there were only 1,500 km of motorway in the Community, almost entirely in West Germany, while by 1966 there were nearly 7,000 km, almost a half in Germany and a further third in Italy.[4] The system is designed primarily to connect together the Community's great industrial regions, and naturally uses many basic routeways which are followed also by other means of transport, but they are providing new trunk connections from the Middle Rhinelands to south-east Germany, across the Apennines from Bologna to Leghorn and from Florence to Rome. Besides this they are being used as instruments in the overall regional policy, and by extending the Autostrada del Sole right into the toe of Italy and exempting it from the tolls which are being levied on all the other Italian motorways, it is hoped to stimulate economic activity in the Mezzogiorno (See Chapter 5).

The motorways are also being planned in a way that the railways never were, in order to facilitate fast, through travel from one country to another, and to this end the national plans are being carefully concerted. The Dutch motorway from Rotterdam to Arnhem now meets a German autobahn at the frontier which provides through communication on to the Ruhr, and similarly the Antwerp-Liège motorway goes on to join the German system at Aachen.

The greatest single challenge to the success of the Community in the transport sector is without doubt the barrier of mountains which has through history isolated Italy from northern Europe. With Italy steadily becoming more closely associated with its northern neighbours, priority has been given to the need to overcome the physical problem of movement, and to this end the autostrada northward from Milan connects through Switzerland with the Mannheim-Basle autobahn, and another is planned over the Brenner pass to link the Autostrada del Sole with the German system just south of Munich. However, one of the greatest steps forward in trans-Alpine road communication came in 1964 with the opening of the Great St Bernard Tunnel and this was followed in 1966 by another under

Mont Blanc.[5] These two achievements would not have been possible without a close coordination of the transport policies of the French and Italian governments acting within the overall framework of the Community transport blueprint. By piercing the Alps in this way,

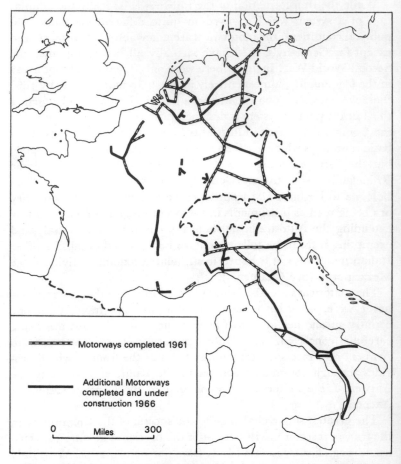

Fig. 5. Motorways completed and under construction, 1961 and 1966.

the north of Italy has for the first time been plugged directly to the Paris-Marseilles axis by trunk roads, and this and other transport improvements have now provided a direct link between the central industrial areas of France and Italy.

The special value of water transport is for the movement of raw materials in bulk and it is a great advantage to all industrial regions to have canal or river connections. In 1955, as part of a general

24

settlement in which the Saar was handed back by France to Germany, the two countries agreed to be jointly responsible for canalizing the Moselle river so as to link the Lorraine industrial area with the Rhine navigation.[6] The stretch from Coblenz to Thionville, a distance of 260 km was finally opened in 1964 to vessels of up to 1,500 tons. This is of especial value to Lorraine which has suffered from the lack of cheap transport, especially for coal from the Ruhr. In 1966 the traffic of the waterway was already 5 million tons, a quarter as much as that using the Seine, France's most important inland waterway, and it is expected to double over the next few years. Much of this increase has been for Luxembourg which now for the first time has access to water transport on a significant scale, and has opened an inland port at Mertert-Grevenmacher to take advantage of this.[7]

Another project of importance is the Main-Danube canal which will make Nuremberg into an inland port. In northern Italy the Po and its associated waterways are to be extended to take European standard vessels of 1,350 tons as far as Milan, and there is a proposed connection with Switzerland which would bring Italian water transport to within 200 km of the Rhine.[8] Numerous other waterways are, of course, being constructed and improved throughout the Community, but of especial long-term importance is the trunk routes plan which aims to connect the North Sea and the Mediterranean via Antwerp, the Canal de l'Est, the Rhône-Saône and Marseilles by a waterway able to take the European standard vessels. There is also the extension of the Rhône canal and the complete rebuilding of the Rhône-Rhine canal which is now in progress and will link the Rhine directly with the Mediterranean for vessels of the same size.[9] Thus the Rhône corridor is becoming steadily more important as the main water transport artery from the Mediterreanean to the north of the Community, and this explains the growing importance of Marseilles as an entrepôt for a large part of the continent.

One of the most revolutionary of all developments in transport, and one which would not have been likely had it not been for the existence of the Community, has been the construction of long-distance pipelines for crude oil, refined petroleum and natural gas. The main crude oil pipelines are those going northward from the Rhône delta, Genoa, and Trieste, and those leading into the interior from Rotterdam and Emden.[10] They all converge on south Germany and the Middle Rhinelands, the landlocked heart of the Community, which has now become a major centre of oil refining (See Chapter

25

3). The movement of oil products is generally over smaller distances, and the most important are from the Seine estuary refineries to Paris and from the Ligurian coast to the upper Po industrial area.

Another development which has taken place since the establishment of the Community is the long distance transmission of electricity, and the most important lines are from the Alps and Pyrenees to Paris and from south Germany and Switzerland to the Ruhr and Rhinelands. These developments will be considered in more detail in the next chapter.

It will be apparent from this that while the Community is spanned by a mesh of lines of communication, both old and new, and each having its own particular uses, it is possible to distinguish a number of routes which on account of the quantity of material carried and the variety of means used stand out as being of more than average importance (Fig. 6). The most important such route is without question that following the Rhine, and in 1962 the waterway between Basle and Rotterdam alone carried 189 million tons of cargo, a quarter that of all the railways in the Six. The intensity of this traffic can be seen from the fact that while its total length is 840 km, that of the Community's railways is 92,000 km, and throughout the zone Hamburg-Basle-Dunkirk Rhine shipping is a major competitor with road and rail carriers.[11] Besides the waterway the route is followed closely by roads and railways, and rather less closely by motorways, pipelines, and electricity transmission lines. While the older routes were attracted by the ease of movement along this incomparable avenue into the centre of the continent, the newer ones which have recently joined them are less dependent on the nature of the relief, and follow it because it joins together some of the Community's largest industrial regions. Besides this there are the major navigable tributaries, the Moselle, Herne, Main, and Neckar, which are all able to take European standard vessels and are followed, like the Rhine, by other means of transport. These and other routes lead to the coasts and connect the whole system with other regions. To the north, a pipeline, motorway, and waterway branch out from the Ruhr to the German North Sea coast, and to the west a variety of communications, many of them not nearly adequate, connect with the Community's second largest port, Antwerp. While, as seen already, the development of these 'branch lines' was originally bound up with political factors, they are now useful for siphoning off trade from the congested Rhinemouth at Rotterdam.

To the south, as we have seen, the Rhône-Saône corridor has emerged, or rather re-emerged, as a major connection between the

26

Mediterranean and the Rhinelands, and the trans-Alpine routes between Germany and Italy through Switzerland and Austria now handle a great deal of trade. The whole of this vast area of the central Community stretching from the North Sea to the Mediterranean is

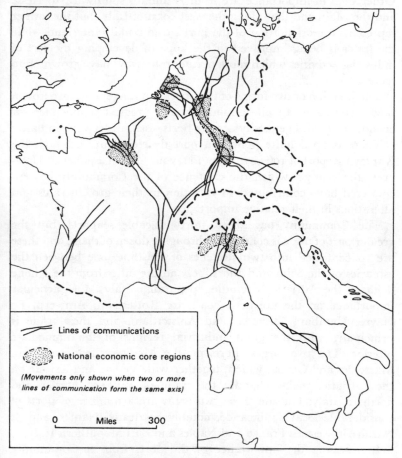

Lines of communications

National economic core regions

(Movements only shown when two or more lines of communication form the same axis)

0   Miles   300

Fig. 6. Principal axes of communication.

bound together by through lines of communication which radiate from the Middle Rhinelands, and this region has now become the pivot for the Community's communications system, a function which has in many ways been emphasized by the developments of the last decade.

The only independent axis with a similar variety and quantity of transport operations is the lower Seine to Paris which handles the maritime trade of France's core region. Since this route continues in attenuated form into the Rhône corridor, this latter has the dual function of funnel for the Mediterranean trade of Paris over the Langres plateau and that of the Rhineland through the Belfort gap. Other lines of importance are from Hamburg southward to Hesse and the Main and that along the west coast of Italy, but the former represents a reorientation of the port's traditional hinterland while the latter is being improved in the hope of developing the sort of industrial activities which more mature routeways have grown up to serve.

The junction of two forms of transport can range in nature from a power station to an oil terminal, but of greatest significance for economic activity generally are the ports—sea, waterway, and air.

There is no definite policy on port development, although the Kapteyn Report of 1962 came out in favour of such a policy.[12] However, the changes which the existence of the Community has encouraged have contributed to variation in their growth rates and alterations in their relative importance.

The Community has about thirty sizeable seaports, but the greater part of trade is conducted through a dozen of them, and these are concentrated into two stretches of coastline, one between the estuaries of the Seine and the Elbe, and the other from the Rhône delta to the Adriatic (excluding peninsular Italy). Of particular importance on the northern coast are Rotterdam, Antwerp, Le Havre, Hamburg, Bremen, and Amsterdam, and their trade is principally with the great industrial regions of the immediate interior. The two largest ports on the Mediterranean coast are Marseilles and Genoa, which, together with Venice and Trieste on the Adriatic, mainly handle the trade of southern France and northern Italy. Outside these two areas are a number of ports of considerable local significance, notably Bordeaux, Nantes, and St Nazaire in western France and Naples and Bari in southern Italy.

In assessing the importance of the ports from a Community standpoint it is possible to divide them into two categories—the regional ports and the 'euroports'. The former have grown up to serve the needs of limited areas, normally consisting of one part of the national territory in which they are situated; the 'euroports' on the other hand serve a much larger area cutting across national frontiers and frequently in competition with the regional ports.

The establishment of the Community has created the conditions in which the euroports have thrived, and as a consequence the functions they perform have been on the increase. The two great euroports which pre-dated the Community are Rotterdam at the mouth of the Rhine and Antwerp on the Scheldt. Located at Western Europe's front door, they are able to handle a large proportion of its trade with ease. In 1965 Rotterdam alone handled 122·7 million tons of cargo, more than any other port in the world, and nearly a threefold increase since 1938.[13] This compares with a general increase of 2·8 times in the volume of trade handled by the Community's twelve principal ports over the same period, and the port has been able to cope with the increase through an extensive modernization programme notably the building of the appropriately named Europoort a little downstream on the Nieuwe Waterweg. Rotterdam's hinterland is fundamentally the Rhine basin, with which it is connected by a variety of means from the oldest of them all, the river itself, to the new motorways and crude oil pipelines.[14]

Antwerp, the Community's second port, handled only a half as much cargo as Rotterdam in 1965, but like the latter this was a threefold increase over 1938. While it does not have its great neighbour's advantage of direct water connections with the Rhine, there are now fast road and rail links with Cologne and the Ruhr. Its hinterland is by no means coterminous with that of Rotterdam, since it is basically the principal port for Belgium and for part of northern France, but it is now in direct competition with Rotterdam for the Rhineland trade.

The edges of the Community's principal trading coastline are held by Hamburg and Le Havre, which have grown to importance as the major ports serving their respective capital cities. The change in geographical values brought about the the division of Germany and the cutting off of Hamburg from its hinterland has been detrimental to the port's development, and further to this its very peripheral location in relation to the centres of economic activity in the Community has proved a considerable disadvantage and put its future in jeopardy.[15] Although still one of the Community's major ports and West Germany's main liner terminal, its trade has increased by only one-third since 1938 and it is losing ground to the Rhine ports. In contrast to this Le Havre has tripled its goods turnover since 1938, and while before the Second World War it handled only one-third that of Hamburg, it has now very nearly caught up with it.

Of the other northern ports, the largest is Bremen which, although very near to Hamburg, has a different natural hinterland based on the Weser drainage area. It is far from being ideally located for Community trade but improvements to its facilities and good communications with the Ruhr have enabled a considerable expansion to take place. The fortunes of Dunkirk have changed in the opposite direction from those of the German North Sea ports, and her formerly peripheral location on the Franco-Belgian frontier has been converted into a very central one for the expanding Pas de Calais and Flanders areas.

Table 4. Cargo handled by the twelve principal ports of the European Community, 1938 and 1965.

	1938		1965	
	Total cargo in 1000s tons	*% of twelve ports total*	*Total cargo in 1000s tons*	*% of total for twelve ports*
Rotterdam	46,371	30·2	122,705	28·5
Antwerp	23,579	15·3	59,440	14·0
Marseilles	9,955	6·5	56,823	13·4
Hamburg	25,795	16·7	35,267	8·3
Genoa	7,274	4·7	34,039	8·0
Le Havre	6,667	4·4	38,036	6·6
Bremen	8,994	5·9	17,494	4·1
Dunkirk	4,244	2·8	16,271	3·8
Naples	2,868	1·9	15,449	3·7
Venice	4,176	2·7	14,627	3·4
Amsterdam	5,655	3·7	13,907	3·3
Rouen	7,702	5·0	10,573	2·5

(Source: J. Bird, *The Geographical Journal*)

The two great ports of the Mediterranean coast, Marseilles and Genoa, with a combined turnover of over 90 million tons, are now respectively third and fourth largest in the Community. Both have increased their trade, fivefold in the case of Genoa and nearly sixfold in that of Marseilles since 1938, much larger increases than those of any other principal port in the Community. This has been due in the case of Marseilles to the increase in trade with northern Europe along the Rhône corridor, and in the case of Genoa to a combination of the booming conditions in the north Italian industrial area and the great improvements in trans-Alpine communications. These two are essentially euroports, and this applies especially to Marseilles which, lacking a large industrial area in its immediate hinterland, but with an excellent natural routeway to northern Europe, is bidding fair to become the Rotterdam of the Mediterranean. Genoa has been handicapped in this by the inadequate space for expansion and the difficulties of crossing the Alps, but these problems are now being tackled, the former by the opening of the new inland port at Rivalta Scrivia some 55 km to the north across the Apennines from which goods are distributed over northern Italy.[16] We have already seen how trans-Alpine communications are improving and this is helping to increase Genoa's trade with northern Europe. As to the two Adriatic ports, Venice on a smaller scale than Genoa handles a great deal of trade with the upper Po valley and it is well located to do this. The trans-Alpine connections of Trieste were given a fillip in 1967 with the opening of the crude oil pipeline to Ingolstadt.

No survey of ports, however brief, would be complete without mentioning the inland ports which are of such importance in the Community. Those of real significance are almost entirely confined within an area bounded by the lower Seine, Strasbourg and the Elbe which contains the bulk of the navigable rivers and canals. The most important are those of the Rhine, particularly Duisburg which serves the Ruhr and Ludwigshafen-Mannheim at the junction of the Rhine and the Neckar. Also of great importance is Strasbourg whose situation on one of the Community's internal frontiers has, like that of Dunkirk, been turned to advantage. It is now the second inland port of France, after Paris, and is very central to the main areas of economic expansion in the Community. Paris was until quite recently the largest port of any kind in France, but now a larger volume of goods is handled at both Le Havre and Marseilles. It remains, however, of great significance as a distribution point for the whole of north-eastern France.

Although air transport is making a steadily greater contribution to the movement of freight, the amount is but a small percentage of that transported by any one of the major surface methods. It is handicapped by its limited capacity and flexibility together with the relatively high freight charges, and its main advantages are its security and speed of delivery. It is, therefore, most useful for goods of high value and those which have to be moved quickly.

The overall distribution of airports is a very different one from that of seaports, and only a few of the latter have significant air connections. The Community's two largest ports, Rotterdam and Antwerp, both have air services but these are small compared with those of the main national airports, and this is true also of the other countries. Airports are for the most part situated in the interior, since air journeys do not have to be interrupted at the coasts, and so are able to terminate in places which are best located to suit the maximum demand. In the Community, with the sole exception of West Germany, the largest airports of each country are those of its capital city. The attraction of the capital is twofold: with its political, financial, and business concentration it has normally the largest number of people who are likely to want to make use of air transport, and secondly, being either the hub of the national transport system, or one of its most important centres, it is relatively accessible for passengers coming from a wide area.

In the small countries of the Benelux Union, the capital's airport has an absolute dominance, but in the case of the larger countries subsidiary centres have developed to cater for regional needs. While Rome has by far the largest air traffic in Italy, Milan has a large airport serving the north, and in France the same is true of Lyons and Marseilles. Paris is by far the largest air traffic centre in the whole Community, and its two main airports of Orly and Le Bourget have a variety of European and world services unmatched elsewhere in the Six. Besides catering for the needs of the Community's largest city, it is important as a major centre for air transport throughout Western Europe.

In Germany the federal capital, Bonn, is quite a small town which shares its airport with nearby Cologne, and the regions are catered for by large airports located in the principal cities. The country's largest airport is at Frankfurt, which because of its central location has also become an important road and rail centre. In West Germany its function is now analogous to that performed by the national airports in the other countries, and its central location has also made it an important junction in the West European air services generally.

The needs of the tourist trade have also been responsible for the growth of airports in many places, notably Nice and Naples and many smaller places particularly in Italy and the south of France.

As a whole the Community's transport system is dominated by north-south trunk lines of communication which serve the major internal and external movements of trade. The most important of these is the Rhine axis, around which has grown up an intricate pattern of communications which connect it with other parts of the Community. The penetration of the central mountain divide by more efficient means of communication is making it steadily less of an obstacle to contacts between the north and the south, and this is pushing the Rhine axis across the Alps into northern Italy and increasing its contacts via the Rhône-Saône with the French Mediterranean.

The main technical change of importance to the transport pattern as a whole is the increasing tendency of the conventional methods of transport such as rail and canal to specialize in certain types of goods, together with the development of entirely new methods such as pipelines and transmission lines which is helping to make this specialization possible. This is having the dual effect of further emphasizing the existing basic routeways and at the same time of opening up entirely new ones.

Economic necessity coupled with conscious Community policy is now in process of creating a homogeneous system out of the six national ones. Without this the fusing of the economies, which it is the intention of the Treaty of Rome to bring about, can be no more than a pipe dream. Some of the most important projects—the Moselle canalization, the trans-Alpine and trans-Europe pipelines and the Alpine tunnels—have been brought about by concerted action to meet existing economic needs. However, transport is also being used as an instrument of policy, and as such it is one of the Community's most powerful weapons in guiding the direction of economic growth in the future.

3 The Energy Revolution

The most essential requirement of every industrial country is a readily available supply of energy, and while raw materials can be varied and substituted, energy in one form or another is needed in all manufacturing processes. Until well into the present century in the countries of the European Community this meant one thing: coal. It was used by most industries, powered the railways and the ships which moved their products, and was the main domestic fuel of the work people. By the early years of the twentieth century gas and electricity were becoming of considerable importance, but they too were mostly converted forms of coal energy. As recently as 1952, when the Coal and Steel Community came into being, nine-tenths of the home-produced power and two-thirds of that consumed was derived from coal. Since then, however, the share of coal has been falling rapidly and by 1966 it was down to two-thirds of home production and only one-third of consumption. Over this period total energy requirements had nearly doubled from 353 to 626 million tons coal equivalent, but the output of coal decreased from 244 to 210 million tons.[1]

In spite of the coal industry's contraction, demand has of late been falling even more rapidly than output and unsold stocks have been rising. While in 1964 these were 14 million tons, by 1965 they had risen to 26 million and by 1966 to 50 million.[2] There are many reasons for this unfavourable change in the fortunes of the fuel which is still the Community's most important source of home-produced power, and one of these is the disposition of the reserves. About two-thirds of all coal mined in the Community is from West Germany, and nearly a quarter from France, while the bulk of the remainder is Belgian. Of the other three countries, the Dutch have one small coalfield, Italy a few minute ones, and Luxembourg none at all. In the coal age this meant that Italy had to bring in practically all her fuel, mostly from Europe's two great surplus producers, Great Britain and Germany, while the output of France and the Netherlands was totally insufficient to meet their needs, and they had to supplement it with large imports. These countries have therefore been very interested in finding substitutes, particularly ones which involve the use of home resources.

The 'twentieth century fuels', led by gas, oil, and hydroelectricity, have been cutting deeply into traditional markets besides creating their own new ones. In all forms of transport for instance, the use of coal-generated steam power has been giving place to the oil-fired internal combustion engine and to electric power. Not only are oil fuels adapted to these engines in a way in which coal is not, but also in the Community imported oil has the advantage of being cheaper than coal. Paradoxically coal has also suffered from the increased efficiency with which it can now be used. In some of its largest markets, for example the generation of thermal electricity, a far smaller amount of coal is now required to produce a given quantity of power than in the past.

Furthermore, imported coal can frequently be obtained at a lower price than that which is home-produced. Output per miner in the United States is five to seven times the Community average, and American coal can be landed at European ports at $11 to $12 per ton, as compared with the average pithead prices in the Community of $15 to $17.[3] In 1965 29 million tons was imported, two-thirds of it from the United States, with most of the remainder coming from Eastern Europe and the United Kingdom.

The greater part of the Community's coal reserves are found in a west-east belt stretching from Northern France through the Low Countries into West Germany (Fig. 7). This consists of the Franco-Belgian, Kempenland, South Limburg, Aachen and Ruhr coalfields, and about 80 per cent of the total Community output is extracted from it, while the Saar-Lorraine basin to the south is an important outlier which accounts for a further 13 per cent. By far the most important single coalfield is the Ruhr which produced 116 million tons in 1965, four-fifths of West Germany's total and over a half that of the Community. The thick northward-dipping seams contain a variety of types and qualities of coal which by European standards are easy to exploit, and this is reflected in the output of 2,895 kg per manshift in 1965, one of the highest in the Community (Table 5). Western Europe's largest heavy industrial region is situated for the most part above this coalfield and it has thus the added advantage of a large local market. After increasing throughout the

35

1950s, output stabilized in the early 1960s at about 120 million tons per annum, but because of the slackening demand and uncompetitive costs it has now started to fall again.[4] Nearby in the vicinity of

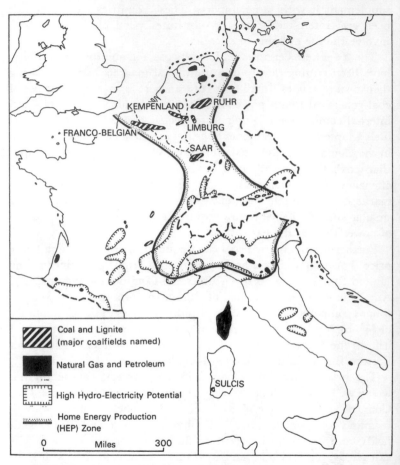

Fig. 7. Sources of energy.

Cologne is the Community's principal lignite mining region, which produces the greater part of the 100 million tons of this fuel obtained annually. This does not make such a large contribution to energy supplies as might be thought, since it has a low calorific value and is equivalent only to about 30 million tons of coal.

The second largest field is the Franco-Belgian, which in 1965 produced 36 million tons, 26 million of these coming from Northern France and 10 million from Southern Belgium. During the last decade output has been decreasing more rapidly here than in almost any other field in the Community, particularly in the Belgian section where it has been halved since the early 1950s. This coalfield is far less favoured than the Ruhr both in the quality and variety of the coal and in the ease with which it can be extracted. Over-manning, high wage costs, and the retention of uneconomic pits have also added to its problems (Table 5). In 1965 southern Belgium with only one-eleventh the output of the Ruhr had 47 mines in operation, half the number operating in the larger field. The same sort of conditions are found in the French Nord, and output here has been steadily phased down.

Table 5. Output and Productivity in the Coal Industry 1965

	Total Output (mill. tons)	Output per manshift (kg)	Number of pits
Ruhr	116	2,895	89
Aachen	8	2,221	6
Lower Saxony	2	2,188	2
Saar	14	2,740	9
Nord/Pas de Calais	25	1,662	38
Lorraine	16	3,239	7
Centre-Midi (mainly Massif Central)	10	2,044	25
Italy	0·3	2,906	1
Netherlands	12	2,253	12
Kempenland	10	2,102	7
South Belgium	10	1,697	47

(Source: Energy Statistics 1950–65. Statistical Office of the European Communities)

In contrast to the difficulties faced by their larger neighbours, the smaller coalfields of the central belt have been showing considerable buoyancy, and in Kempenland and Aachen output has actually continued to increase. Kempenland's output of 9·7 million tons in 1965 nearly equalled that of South Belgium, while ten years earlier it had been only a half that of its large neighbour. Since 1964 however it has begun to decline slightly in face of competition, and in 1965 for the first time over 1 million tons were left unsold. Output is now also declining in the Dutch Limburg field which maintained an increase until the early 1960s. Although it is the country's only coalfield, it is now facing competition from the recently discovered natural gas resources of Groningen and Guelderland.

Since the establishment of the Community, the two parts of the

Saar-Lorraine coalfield have developed very differently. The Saar has problems common to long-exploited coalfields everywhere, and productivity remains below the German average although above that of the Community as a whole. Although the industry has been

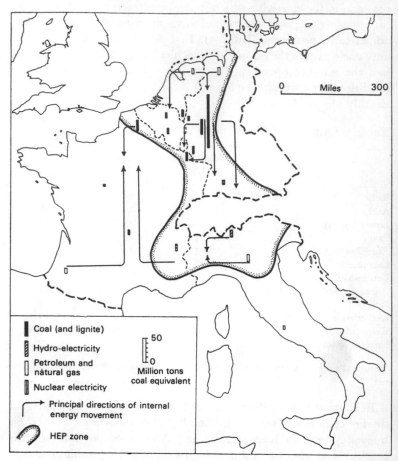

Fig. 8. Home production of primary energy.

reorganized and the number of mines in operation halved, in the last ten years output has been steadily decreasing. By contrast, Lorraine, where in 1938 only 6·8 million tons was extracted, overtook the Saar in 1963 and had an output of 15·5 million tons in 1965. It now has the highest productivity of any coalfield in the Community, benefiting both from the use of new techniques and the expansion of the adjacent industrial region.

Practically all the 5 per cent of the Community's coal extracted outside the central belt and its outlier is from the Massif Central. In 1955 its output of 13 million tons was a quarter of the French total, but by 1965 it had fallen to 10 million, only a fifth of the national production. The region's coalfields are small and dispersed, mostly of indifferent quality and remote from the high consumption areas. They achieved considerable importance in an age when there was no alternative to coal, and when the country's best supplies suffered the disadvantage of being both peripheral and vulnerable. The change brought about by the establishment of the Community has now made the Massif Central itself peripheral, and the technical developments which have accompanied this have made its decline inevitable.

The Coal and Steel Community itself has become a direct agent in the process of change, and its existence has radically altered the conditions within which the industry now operates. The policy of the High Authority has had two principal aims. The first has been to control and guide the inevitable decline of the coal industry and to ensure that the process will cause as little disruption as possible to the economy as a whole and minimize the hardship to those involved. Its second aim has been to help plan output so as to ensure that coal is mined in the most efficient way and at prices which are competitive with those of other fuels. The target for 1970 is only 190 million tons, a decrease of nearly one-third on the 1961 output.[5] The phased reduction is being brought about both by the economic necessity of modernizing production, as well as by the direct intervention of the High Authority and of national governments. The High Authority itself has provided grants for retraining schemes, direct grants to unemployed miners, and aid to industrialists in setting up new works in decaying mining areas (See Chapter 5). Altogether between 1954 and 1966 some 270,000 workers have been helped in this way, the Franco-Belgian and Massif Central coalfields having been particularly large recipients of Community aid. Besides this, grants have been awarded for research into new uses for coal and its by-products and into new methods of extraction.[6]

The basic achievement of the ECSC is that it has created one large market for coal and its products where six existed before, but in spite of this there has been no sustained increase in the intra-Community coal trade. In 1952 this was 15 million tons and by 1965 it had risen to a little over 16 million. Of this over two-thirds—12 million tons— came from Germany alone, and most of it went to the Low Countries (6 million) and to France (5½ million). The other five countries are on balance importers of Community coal, the largest being France which gets over one eighth of her supplies from other Community countries.

A notable development of another sort is that since the Community came into being, Italy has almost stopped buying at all from her partners and has switched to bulk imports of American and, to a certain extent, of Russian coal (Table 6). All the other Community countries, except Luxembourg, also import large quantities from America, but the relative importance of this trade varies. Belgium has tripled her imports over the last fifteen years but most of the increase comes from the adjacent German and Dutch fields. The Dutch increase of about one third over the same period has also been made up mainly of German coal. The quantity and pattern of German and French imports have tended to remain fairly stable but while six-sevenths of German imports are from the United States, two-thirds of the French are from Community countries, and she places only a small reliance on supplies of American coal.

Table 6. Imports and Exports of Coal of ECSC Countries, 1965

	Exports into ECSC Countries	Imports from ECSC Countries	Imports from Non-ECSC Countries
	Millons tons		
West Germany	11·9	1·0	7·6
France	0·7	7·0	5·0
Italy	—	0·4	10·2
Belgium	1·6	4·1	2·7
Netherlands	2·0	3·7	3·5
Luxembourg	—	0·1	—
Total	16·2	16·3	29·0

(Source: Energy Statistics 1950–65. Statistical Office of the European Communities)

Increases in the intra-Community trade have been particularly marked in the case of coalfields near to the national frontiers. Before the Community was established almost all Aachen's coal went to the German market, and the Benelux countries bought only 15 per cent of it, but some years later 33 per cent of it went to them.[7] Similarly the sales of Dutch Limburg to adjacent Belgium and Germany have gone up, and an important contributory factor in this and other developments has been the abolition of frontier price tapering. Between 1952 and 1962, for example, the cost of transporting coke from the Ruhr to Lorraine decreased by 30 per cent, and over the same period the trade in coal showed considerable stability, and that in coke increased appreciably.[8] This important trade was further stimulated by the completion of the Moselle canalization in 1964, since when increasing quantities have been going by water.

The heady wind of unrestrained competition was too much all at once for the less efficient coalfields, and this was particularly the case in southern Belgium, which, besides having high operating costs, is so located as to be very vulnerable to competition from more successful neighbours such as the Ruhr. The High Authority therefore waived its rules in the case of Belgium, and over the period from 1959–63 permitted the reestablishment of protection while modernization was taking place. Over the years from 1950–65 102 mines were closed, almost entirely in the southern fields, but since 1965 closures have begun to spread to the Kempenland.

The increased competition which the Community has encouraged, together with the decreasing importance of coal, have been combining to alter the emphasis in the geographical pattern of mining. The coalfields of the central area in which output is still increasing, or has only recently begun to decrease, are the Ruhr, Kempenland, Aachen, and Lorraine. In the next few years the only two Community fields in which output is expected to increase are Lorraine and Aachen, with the exception of the special case of Sulcis in Sardinia (See page 90). In the Ruhr itself there has been a shift of emphasis in output from the east towards the west, and consequently the Community's most flourishing mining area now follows a north-south axis embracing the coalfields from the Ruhr to Lorraine, most of which have for economic and strategic reasons been underexploited in the past. They are, therefore, in large measure free of the social and economic problems which beset the older coalfields while at the same time being central to the new economic area and close to some of its largest markets.

This geographical contraction mirrors the contraction in the uses of coal which is now in competition with so many other sources of energy, and has become over the last decade more and more a specialist fuel. While its use has decreased markedly in all forms of transport, its greatest importance now is for conversion into secondary energy. In 1965 182 million tons or 70 per cent of the total output were used for this purpose. When the Community was established only 60 per cent of the output was so used. Traditionally power stations and gas works are consumer-orientated industries, and the coal is moved to them by rail or water. Recent developments have been the conversion into gas and electricity at the pithead or nearby, and the transporting of the derived energy by long-distance electricity transmission or pipelines. The capacity of the pithead power stations has been increasing rapidly in order to satisfy the growing demand for cheap electricity. This has been particularly true in West Germany, where output more than doubled in the period 1955–66 to a total of 5,244 MW. In the former year the country was contributing 46 per cent of the total Community potential, while by 1966 this had become 53 per cent, and the Ruhr capacity increased during the period by 140 per cent, the highest in the Community, making it responsible for four-fifths of the German total. In the other German fields and in South Belgium capacity also more than doubled, but by contrast the rise in Dutch and French potential was much lower. In Lorraine there was an increase of only a half, and in the Massif Central only one-fifth.

Table 7. Capacity in Megawatts of Pithead Power Stations by Coalfield

	1955	1966
West Germany	2,254	5,244
Ruhr	1,727	4,153
Other German	527	1,091
Belgium	641	1,275
Kempenland	253	409
Southern Belgium	388	866
Netherlands (Limburg)	283	470
France	1,790	2,686
Nord/Pas de Calais	856	1,406
Lorraine	475	723
Centre/Midi (mainly Massif Central)	459	557
Community	4,968	9,675

(Source: Investment in the Community Coalmining and Iron and Steel Industries ECSC 1966)

It will be remembered that in the days when coal dominated the energy scene, most of the electricity and gas used in the Community countries was derived from it, but now the home production of both comes also from a number of other sources, particularly hydro and nuclear electricity together with natural gas. These make up most of the third of indigenous energy which now comes from sources other than coal, and together with the small home output of petroleum they are responsible for the great diversification in energy production which has taken place since the Second World War.

In order to generate hydroelectricity, the only essential raw material is plenty of water, but there are many extras which can turn it from an uneconomic luxury into one of the cheapest forms of power available. The most important of these are mountains to give a natural head of water, deep valleys into which it can be impounded, and impervious rocks to keep as much of it as possible on the surface. Added advantages are natural reservoirs and a moderate climate in which the water will neither freeze nor evaporate excessively.

The mountainous regions which are likely to be most suitable for producing hydroelectric power have not in the past developed a very high level of economic activity in other fields, and so consumption in the vicinity of the generating stations is usually small. The disadvantages of generating electricity in this way are, therefore, not only the high capital cost of the installations but the long distances over which it may have to be transmitted. Production is consequently most attractive in those countries which both possess the necessary physical conditions and at the same time lack other readily exploitable sources of home energy.

France and Italy are the two countries in the Community which best combine these conditions, and in 1965 they were together responsible for nearly nine-tenths of the 105,502 GWh produced. Right up to the present day these two countries have been at a considerable disadvantage industrially, when compared with Germany and Belgium, because of the inadequacy of their home coal supplies to meet internal demands. This has been particularly so with Italy which, possessing virtually no coal, produced only energy to the value of 17 million tons coal equivalent in 1950, one-ninth of the German output in the same year. The high mountains and deep valleys of the Southern Alps are, therefore, a resource of considerable importance, and in the last twenty years she has lost no time in developing their potential. A further advantage is their nearness to the high consumption regions of the north which have a great energy deficit. With 14,297 MW Italy has the largest installed capacity in the Community, and by 1965 it had become her largest single form of home-produced power, accounting for a half of the total energy output and well over a half of the electricity.

France also has long suffered economically from the inability of her own coal reserves to meet her needs, and in recent years hydroelectricity has been helping to make up this deficit.[9] Since the founding of the Community her output has doubled, a rate of increase more rapid than that of either of her two major partners.

Three-quarters of her output comes from the Alps and the Pyrenees which have the same combination of physical advantages as are present in Northern Italy, but have suffered the disadvantage of being remote from the principal energy-consuming regions in the north. In the last decade this situation has changed considerably, and south-east France, 'le coin déshérité' as it used to be called, has been developing rapidly. In 1965 one-fifth of France's energy and nearly one-half of her electricity came from water power.

Table 8. Production of Electrical Energy, 1965 (in GWh)

	Hydro	Nuclear	Conventional Thermal	Total
Germany (FR)	15,143	112	145,300	160,555
France	46,429	897	54,116	101,442
Italy	42,756	3,345	32,141	78,242
Netherlands	—	—	23,657	23,657
Belgium	270	—	20,095	20,365
Luxembourg	904	—	1,316	2,220
Total	105,502	4,354	276,625	386,571

(Source: Basic Statistics of the Community 1966, Statistical Office of the European Communities)

Almost all the remaining tenth of Community output comes from Germany, but with its huge reserves of coal for transforming into thermal and its less favourable conditions for making hydroelectricity, there is naturally less enthusiasm for developing potential resources. Almost all the 15,000 GWh generated in 1965 came from the mountainous south-east of the country and represented only 3 per cent of the country's energy output.

In the Low Countries, as one might expect, it is even less important than is home raised coal in Italy, but it is interesting that in Luxembourg it is the only home source of energy, and in 1965 nearly 1,000 GWh was generated at Vianden on the River Our, a project completed in 1963 with funds from the European Investment Bank (See Chapter 5). In spite of this it only provides a fraction of the Duchy's needs, which are satisfied almost exclusively by German coal and imports of refined oil.

A close comparison can be made between the production of hydro-electric power and nuclear power in the Community, although the latter is by far the less developed of the two. Both have the disadvantage of enormously high capital costs, both need plenty of water, and both are especially attractive to France and Italy for similar reasons. However, while hydroelectricity either can or cannot be generated in a given set of physical conditions, the sites for nuclear power production are nothing like so closely determined, and since uranium can be transported easily, little more than water and ample space is essential. With an annual output of about 1,000 tons, the Community has practically enough uranium to meet its own needs, and the main sources of supply are the Limoges and Vendée regions of western France and the Massif Central.

Ninety-eight per cent of the 4,354 GWh of nuclear electricity generated in the Community in 1965 came from Italy and France together, with Italy alone generating three-quarters of it. This is all the more remarkable when one considers that the country did not start production until 1963 when the output was only 296 GWh. Producing as she does less than 30 per cent of her own energy requirements, Italy has a particular interest in all new energy sources, and her industry has in the last few years reached the technical level where she is able to build successful nuclear installations. The whole output comes from only three power stations, two of which, Latina and Garigliano, are situated in the underdeveloped region south of Rome, while in contrast the other, Trino Vercelate, is just west of Milan in the economic heart of the country.[10]

France was the first of the Six to produce nuclear power, which she did in 1957, and she remained the only one until the early 1960s. This was brought about by the lead which she built up in research after the war when both Germany and Italy were very weak, and which she succeeded in maintaining throughout the 1950s. It is made especially attractive by her home reserves of uranium coupled with her serious energy deficit. The two largest power stations, Chinon and St. Laurent-des-Eaux, are both on the Loire in an area deficient in other sources of power and lagging in industrial growth, and there are others at Chooz near the Nord industrial region and Marcoule on the lower Rhône, together with important research stations in the Paris area and in south-east France. The general locational pattern is very similar to that of Italy in its intentionally wide dispersal over the country.

The development of nuclear power in Germany has, as in the case of hydroelectricity, been on a much smaller scale than in France and Italy. This has substantially the same causes together with her late start in nuclear research after the Second World War and its aftermath. The decline of coal as an efficient multi-purpose fuel has in recent years made Germany seek alternatives, but her only large nuclear power station is at Gundremmingen to the west of Munich.

Similarly the Low Countries with their large reserves of fuel and limited capital for research and development have not gone significantly into the nuclear business and have between them only two small power stations.

The overall distribution of nuclear power production is a much wider one than in the case of other sources of primary energy in the Community, since their location is not closely related either to supplies of the fuel or to the consumers. In almost all cases, however, they have been built in regions where there is either a deficit of conventional energy, or where it is hoped that their presence will help stimulate industrial activity. At present it contributes only one per cent of the Community's total electricity, although in the case of Italy it is as high as four per cent. Production is carried out by the national authorities in each case, and Euratom's function is the coordination of research and general policy. It operates four research stations of its own at Ispra in Italy, Geel in Belgium, Petten in the Netherlands and Karlsruhe in West Germany and also participates in national projects.

Until a few years ago it was considered that there was little in the way of natural gas in the Community, but recent prospecting has shown that this is far from being the case. Now substantial natural gasfields are being exploited in parts of central and northern Italy, south-west France and south-east and northern Germany. The most important in prospects if not in present production are the Dutch fields, in particular the one at Slochteren, now known to be one of the largest reserves in the world and only discovered as recently as 1960.

In 1965, 159,333 teracalories of natural gas were produced in the Community, this representing a ninefold increase since 1952 while the output of other types of gas increased by less than a quarter.[11] The most important producers, as with hydroelectricity and nuclear energy, are again Italy and France; Italy alone accounts for some 40 per cent of it. In 1965 76 per cent of all her gas consumption was from this source, while in France the proportion was 38 per cent, but the country whose production is growing fastest is the Netherlands, and a half of her gas consumption now comes from natural gas.

The Community's major gasfields are in the northern plain and in northern Italy, and of the total reserves estimated at 1,500 milliard cubic centimetres, 1,100 of them are in the Netherlands alone, the remainder being in south-west France, northern Germany, and the Po valley. This is a very different distribution from that of hydroelectricity (Fig. 7), and is particularly advantageous in that it provides a local energy supply to places which have in the past suffered from the lack of one.

As a result of the technical problems of transport over long distances, the gas industry in the Community countries has up to now been very market-orientated, and it is the raw material, coal, which has invariably been moved the longest distances. The coming of natural gas has now changed this situation, and long-distance pipelines have been constructed to link the great consuming areas direct with the sources of supply. They are as yet for the most part national systems intended for the supply of the home markets, the French system bringing gas from the south-west to the consuming areas of the north, and the mesh of pipelines in northern Italy supplying the great urban centres. The Dutch are, however, ideally equipped to supply gas to other Community countries both by virtue of their immense reserves and the ease with which it can be transported to the great industrial regions of Belgium and West Germany, and these two countries are now both receiving supplies of it. Germany, although in possession of considerable reserves, has not exploited them to a very great extent, and in 1965 produced about 17 per cent of the Community's natural gas which was only 7 per cent of her own home consumption.

In 1965 the first natural gas was imported in liquid form into the Community from Algeria. This is shipped to a gasification plant on the Seine estuary and from there it is piped to Paris. However, the discovery of so much gas in the Netherlands, and more recently under the North Sea, may well alter the direction of the Community's policy on imports and make it able in the long term to satisfy its wants from European sources.

In 1952 the member countries of the Community were collectively producing some nine-tenths of all their energy requirements, but by 1965 this had gone down to a little over a half. The overwhelming part of this mounting deficit, which in the latter year came to 300 million tons coal equivalent, was made up through imports of oil, now the most important single source of energy and responsible in 1966 for 48 per cent of all that used, while coal now supplies just over 32 per cent.[12] This is a most spectacular change from the position in 1952 when the 42 million tons of crude oil used provided only 18 per cent of the Community's needs and coal at that time was supplying 75 per cent.

The growth in demand for oil has been almost coincidental with the decrease in the demand for coal, due more than anything else to

47

the fuel needs of oil-powered engines and machinery. Not only is oil the fuel for newer forms of transport such as motor vehicles and aircraft, but it has replaced coal for ships and railways as well. For these purposes and for many others, oil is both easier to transport and more convenient to handle than coal, and, in terms of energy produced, it is cheaper than coal in the free market. It has also entered into competition with coal in the production of the derived forms of energy, and there are now many oil-fired power stations. Gas is also an important by-product of oil refining.

Three features of the Community's oil industry have been of great importance in determining its geographical distribution, one being that nineteen in every twenty gallons of oil products are refined from imported crude.[13] While the sources of supply vary from one country to another, the most important are the Middle East and North Africa which between them provide four-fifths of the imports. Since these regions are physically discontinuous with Europe, and distances are considerable, all imports from them at the moment have to be brought in oil tankers. The internal transport of petroleum and its products can be effected most easily and cheaply by river, canal, and pipeline. However, because of the high capital costs of construction the routes have to be chosen carefully and are of necessity inflexible, so the direction of flows has to be thought out well in advance. It is also important to remember that the rapid growth in the importance of petroleum has been due largely to its increasing use in transport of one sort or another. When the Community was established nearly one-half of its total consumption was used for this, although by 1965 this proportion had fallen to one-third, and the importance of petroleum in industry is now increasing.

Prior to the establishment of the Community, oil refineries were concerned almost wholly with supplying their own home markets, but increasingly an overall pattern on a continental scale has begun to evolve related to the needs of the new single market. Since it has only been in the last two decades or so that oil has come to have its present immense importance, the industry has been growing in the new conditions rather than having to adapt itself to them as in the case of coal.

In 1965 there were 101 refineries in the Community, compared with half that number when it was established. Italy leads with 39, followed by Germany with 33 and France with 18. The Netherlands and Belgium have the remaining 11. Of the 244 million tons of crude treated in 1965, Italy was responsible for just over a quarter and

France and Germany for a quarter each. The five Dutch refineries alone have an output of 32 million tons, over a half that of the 33 German ones.

The most noticeable feature of distribution is the concentration of some three-quarters of total capacity around the coasts (Fig. 9). Almost the entire French, Belgian, and Dutch capacities are coastal as are also the overwhelming part of the Italian. This is a direct consequence of the Community's need to import on such a colossal scale, together with the cheapness of refining at coastal sites and distributing the products from there into the interior rather than sending the crude overland to the consuming centres. The most suitable sites for refineries are those with deep water, plenty of available land, and good communications into the interior. Over one-third of the total capacity is on the North Sea-Channel coast between the Seine and the Elbe. Here the major refineries are grouped around those estuaries with rivers leading towards the great interior industrial regions. The Seine estuary group, including the giant Gonfreville refinery with a capacity of 10·6 million tons, sends products by pipeline and river to the Paris region. The Rotterdam group of four refineries is the largest in the Community handling almost the entire Dutch output and it distributes products by river and canal throughout the lower Rhinelands. Likewise Antwerp supplies mid-Belgium, and the refineries on the German North Sea coasts, particularly the Hamburg group with a capacity of 11·5 million tons, supply Schleswig-Holstein and Lower Saxony. The coastal regions themselves use up a lot of the products especially Rotterdam, Amsterdam, and Hamburg with their large concentrations of industry and population.

The other important coast is the Mediterranean which now has nearly a third of the Community's capacity. Particularly important is the section of the Tyrrhenian coast eastwards from the Rhône delta to Sicily where much of the expansion of recent years has taken place. When the Community was established, the whole area was refining only 20 million tons, and a half of this came from the Étang de Berre of south-east France. By 1965 total capacity had gone up to 120 million tons with five-sixths of it from the Italian refineries. This change has been due principally to the accelerating pace of economic growth in Italy since the middle of the 1950s and the consequent increase in demand for oil fuels. It has been accentuated also by the country's chronic home energy deficit and this has contributed to making her now the Community's largest refiner. She has also benefited from the large quantities of oil now coming from

North Africa which can be conveniently refined on the Italian coasts.

The largest Italian refineries are at Genoa, Pavia, Ravenna, and Naples on the mainland and at Milazzo and Priolo in Sicily, all with capacities of over 5 million tons per annum. In south-eastern France the three refineries around the Étang de Berre have a capacity of 18 million tons, one-third of the French total. This is the counterpart of the Seine group of the north and together they handle two-thirds of the country's refining.

In the early 1950s practically all imported crude oil was refined at, or very near to, the coasts, a pattern which had become increasingly established in most of the importing countries of Western Europe. By 1965, however, there were 38 interior refineries with a total throughput of 90 million tons, again nearly one-third of the Community's total. This spectacular increase has been due to the upsurge in demand for oil products coupled with the improvement of quick and cheap transport overland.

The Rhine is the main axis of interior refining, and large oil carriers are able to navigate it all the way from the sea to the Swiss frontier. The biggest centre is the Ruhr, which has had the combined advantages of sea connections via the Rhine and the Dortmund-Ems canal together with a great local demand. Large refineries have been built at Gelsenkirchen, Duisburg, Dinslaken, Godorf and farther upstream at Cologne, and the total capacity of the land of Nordrhein-Westfalen is 33 million tons, all of it connected to the Rhine waterway. Farther upstream still there are refineries at Mannheim, Karlsruhe and Speyer, and in Alsace at Reichstett and Herrlisheim.

An important new development which has given a considerable boost to interior refining has been the construction of pipelines taking the crude from coastal terminals into the interior. The most important ones from the north are the Rotterdam-Gelsenkirchen-Raunheim (RRP) and the Wilhelmshaven-Dinslaken-Wesseling both of which move the crude for refining into the middle Rhinelands (Fig. 9).[14] However, more revolutionary in their implications are those northward from the Mediterranean terminals at Lavera, Genoa, and Trieste. The Lavera one is the 34-inch South-Europe Pipeline (SPLSE) up the Rhône valley to Karlsruhe and Mannheim completed in 1962, and designed to connect with the Rotterdam-Rhine Pipeline (RRP) to provide a through route across the continent from the Mediterranean to the North Sea. Besides this there are the 26-inch Genoa-Aigle-Ingolstadt completed in 1966 and the 40-inch Trieste-Ingolstadt which came into service in 1967. About 40 per cent of all the Community's refineries now receive their crude by pipeline. While the immediate effect of the trans-continental pipelines has been to emphasize further the existing pattern of interior refining, it is also changing it. Refineries have sprung up along the courses of the pipelines, or near to them, and at the inland terminals.

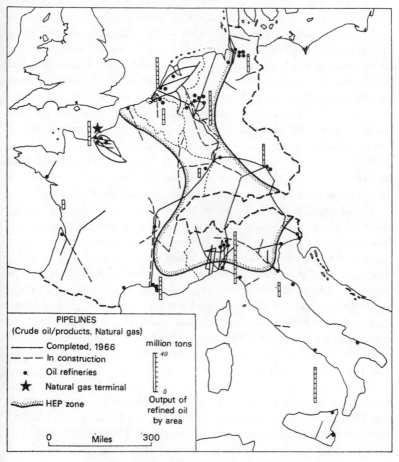

PIPELINES
(Crude oil/products, Natural gas)

——— Completed, 1966
– – – In construction
• Oil refineries
★ Natural gas terminal
~~~~ HEP zone

million tons
40
0
Output of
refined oil
by area

0   Miles   300

Fig. 9. Oil refineries and pipelines.

The new Ingolstadt complex now has five refineries with a total capacity of 11·5 million tons and is geared to supply the large land-locked area of Bavaria and Würtemburg. Besides pipeline connections with the Mediterranean terminals, it has a connection also with Karlsruhe.

The most notable changes in the geography of refining since the

51

establishment of the Community have been the great expansion to new coastal areas, notably those of the Mediterranean, and to certain selected places in the interior. This has been made possible and desirable by the great overall increase in the consumption of oil products and by the establishment of installations with reference to the supply of the Community rather than of the individual parts of it. Thus crude oil is being pumped to Germany from terminals on the Italian coasts, and products from the Dutch refineries are being distributed all over the Rhinelands. It could be argued that even had there been no Community, economic necessity would have brought about similar developments, but in the past political fragmentation has discouraged them, and even when they occurred they have been interfered with by the national governments. The Community is now 'holding the ring' and by so doing producing the conditions in which industries such as oil can plan their activities on a continental scale without fear that their work will be undone. Without this it is unlikely that such developments as we have considered would be of the same kind or of the same magnitude as they have been.

The changes which have taken place in the Community's energy position since 1952 may be summarized thus: while consumption has risen by 85 per cent, home production has risen by only 10 per cent, and output from the major home resource, coal, has actually decreased by 8 per cent. Therefore the two most significant developments have been the increased dependence on imports, which have gone up five and a half times, and the fact that one-third of home output is now from sources other than coal. The most important of these sources are hydroelectricity, output of which has doubled since 1952, natural gas, which has increased five and a half times, and petroleum which has increased eight times.

Most home reserves of oil and gas are in the North European plain, with an outlier in the Po valley; the bulk of the coal is around the Hercynian edges; and the optimum conditions for producing hydroelectricity are in the central mountains. The greatest output of all four together is in a north-south zone stretching from the North Sea coasts to northern Italy, and within this area 95 per cent of the Community's primary energy is produced (Fig. 8). Coal is still by far the most important single source in this Home Energy Production (HEP) zone, although its share is gradually diminishing in favour of the others, and while their areas of production are becoming larger, coal-mining operations are tending to contract towards the middle Rhinelands. The HEP zone has in the past suffered the disadvantage of being astride the boundaries of all six countries, and this has made it geographically peripheral to the national economies as well as strategically vulnerable in case of war. This has hampered the exploitation of its resources either for the benefit of the individual countries or for that of the continent as a whole. Since the establishment of the Community, mutual trade in coal, gas, electricity, and refined oil products has been increasing, particularly in the frontier regions where international transfers are frequently the most obvious way of securing the cheapest power. Not only does the machinery of the Community help this interchange, but its existence makes more acceptable the dependence of one nation upon another for its energy supplies.

Within the Home Energy Production zone the greatest energy-consuming area is westward from the lower Rhine to the North Sea coasts. This is the area in which industries have grown up on and near to the coalfields, but since local coal has lost its monopoly it has to be supplemented by transfers of other forms of energy. Until recently these were made up mainly of imports of oil and oil products from coastal terminals and refineries, but three new developments—the discovery of natural gas nearby, the piping of crude oil from the Mediterranean, and the long distance movement of hydroelectricity from the Alps—have given a fillip to the process of diversification. Even the energy-surplus areas no longer have anything like self-sufficiency since the great demand for different forms of energy has converted every region, whatever its production, into an importer.

Outside the HEP zone the energy requirements are supplied by transfers from the zone itself and by imports. The largest energy-deficit areas are Greater Paris, the eastern part of Lower Saxony from Hamburg to Brunswick, the Lower Rhône and the Rome-Naples area, and most of the energy they get is in the form of electricity and coal. The region with the largest energy deficit of all is Greater Paris, and this imports hydroelectric power and gas by transmission line and pipeline from the south and coal from the north, and its petroleum products come by river and pipeline from the Seine estuary. The development of nuclear electricity is now adding to the energy available in the deficit areas and should eventually make them less dependent on transfers from the HEP zone.

The twin themes of the energy revolution taking place in the Community are diversity and mobility. The basis of this diversification is the movement from coal, which the Community has in abundance, to oil, of which it has relatively little. For a century the central coal belt monopolized the production of industrial energy in the Community countries, but in recent years the discovery of new sources of fuel and the employment of new methods of production have made energy available to areas which in the past have stultified from the lack of it. Together with this there is the ease with which primary energy can be transformed and transported over long

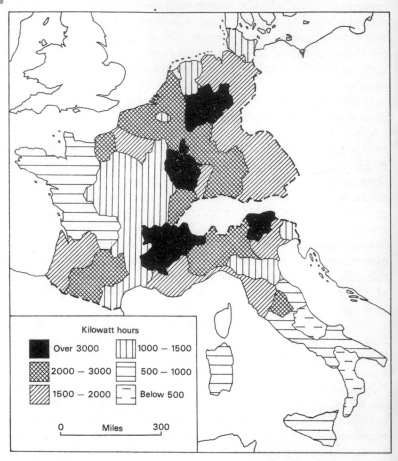

Fig. 10. Electrical energy consumption per capita, 1964.

distances to the consumers in a way which was impossible in the days when coal was the general-purpose fuel and technical problems made it impossible to move its derivatives very far. The meaning of the energy revolution for the economy as a whole is that while in the past industrial activities had to be set up at or near to the source of power, now the power can be moved to the industries.

54

The existence of the Community has produced the conditions in which the energy revolution can take place on a continental scale. It is encouraging the concentration of coal output into the most efficient places and enabling the new sources of power to be harnessed and exploited in the most rational way possible.[15] Locations of new oil refineries are related to the importing facilities and markets of the Community as a whole, and pipelines and transmission lines are based on similar considerations; and while the energy markets still remain overwhelmingly national, their separation is rapidly being eroded away. The Community has, therefore, produced conditions in which a single-energy system can be built, a common policy instituted, and the resources of the six countries utilized for the benefit of them all.

The six countries of the European Community collectively make up one of the great manufacturing areas of the world, and, as can be seen from Table 9, their output is comparable with that of the super-powers. The responsibility for the Community's industry is divided in very unequal proportions between the ECSC and EEC, with the former having only iron and steel and the latter handling all the other manufacturing. This distinction is due to the fact that the first Community in 1952 grouped together what were then the most vital industries in the six countries and put them under international control, and the others were added later when the Economic Community was set up. Here the main features of the distribution of industry in the Community will be examined, and the nature and extent of the changes which have occurred since it first came into being will be evaluated to find out what comparisons and contrasts can be made.

Table 9. Comparative Output of Selected Manufactured Goods, 1965

	EEC	USA	USSR
Pig Iron (mill. tons)	63·2	86·6	66·2
Crude Steel (mill. tons)	86·0	122·0	91·0
Cement (mill. tons)	86·0	62·4	72·4
Motor Vehicles (1,000s)	5,987·7	11,137·8	616·4
Merchant Shipping (1,000 tons)	2,246·0	270·0	Not known
Cotton Yarn (1,000 tons)	1,024·0	1,910·0	1,298·0
Man-made Fibres (1,000 tons)	505·0	727·0	219·0
Plastics (1,000 tons)	3,933·0	5,218·0	821·0

(Source: Basic Statistics of the Community 1966)

Iron and Steel

Although the statement that 'steel is power' may be something of a generalization, the size of a nation's steel industry is as good a guide as any to its standing in the economic league tables, and the buoyancy of this industry reflects that of the economy as a whole. Iron and steel enters into the manufacture of so many things, from armaments to washing machines, that the industry has a special place in the economy of any country. It has already been seen how steel and coal were considered to be the twin bases of national power in the immediate postwar years, and were chosen to constitute the first Community in 1952. Not only were they together of such vital importance, but they were very closely related both economically and geographically, since practically all smelting was done with coal and was carried out at the coal and iron-ore fields.

During the last fifteen years, however, the fortunes of the two have changed in opposite directions, and the association between them has steadily loosened. While coal is providing an ever smaller share of the Community's energy needs, the output of steel has been rising with the overall economic growth of the Six.

Between 1952 and 1966 the Community's steel output more than doubled to 85·2 million tons. This is about the average rate of world increase over this period, and while much smaller than those of Japan and the Soviet Union, it is greater than those of the United States and the United Kingdom. The rates of growth have been different in each of the six countries, and while the increase of the two largest producers, West Germany and France, was rather below the Community average, that of Italy went up four times and her share of the total rose from 9 per cent to 16 per cent. In 1952 Netherlands production was very small, but this increased by five times and at the same time its share of the Community total has doubled to 4 per cent. On the other hand in 1952 BLEU was already responsible for one-fifth of the Community's steel, but with a relatively low rate of increase this has now fallen to one-sixth.

The location of the iron and steel industry in the six countries prior to the establishment of the Community was more than any other single factor related to the presence of coal. Besides having the major fuel for both iron smelting and steelmaking, the carboniferous strata also contain iron ore and limestone, and although the ores are no longer used, the limestone is still important. Besides this, coal, being of low value in proportion to its bulk, is therefore costly to transport very far, and in the past more coal than iron has been required in the smelting process.

This has meant that coalfields have been unrivalled sites for the iron and steel industry, and in the Community has led to concentration on the central coal belt stretching from Pas de Calais to the

57

Ruhr (See Chapter 3). The most suitable conditions were to be found in the Ruhr itself, with its huge quantities of high grade coking coal which is easily and cheaply extracted, together with the adjacent limestone and iron. The area rose to importance during the late nineteenth century, and by 1938 two-thirds of all the steel produced in Germany came from it.[1] The coal measure ores had early proved inadequate, but the Ruhr then had the further advantage of supplies from the nearby Siegerland and could import cheaply up the Rhine which flows past the western edge of the coalfield. This advantage was reinforced by the completion of the Dortmund-Ems canal in 1898, and the Herne canal in 1906. The industry generated its own markets of consuming industries and so further reinforced the advantages of this location.

Table 10. Crude Steel Output in the Community, 1952 and 1966

	Output 1952 (mill. tons)	% of Community Total	Output 1966 (mill. tons)	% of Community Total
Germany (FR)	18·6	45	35·3	42
France	10·9	26	19·6	23
Italy	3·6	9	13·6	16
Netherlands	0·7	2	3·3	4
Belgium	5·1	12	8·9	10
Luxembourg	3·0	7	4·4	5
Total	42·0		85·2	

(Source: Siderurgica, Statistical Office of the European Communities)

Substantial iron and steel industries have also developed on the coalfields of northern France and southern and eastern Belgium. Until recent years almost the whole Belgian output came from its southern coalfield, particularly from the Borinage and the Liège area, and until the end of the nineteenth century the bulk of French output was from the Nord-Pas de Calais region. In both of them conditions are far less ideal than in the Ruhr, since the coals are inferior in quality and more difficult to extract. There is also the transport problem since these regions are not served by waterways to compare with the Rhine, and the French section is particularly badly located for getting cheap ore supplies.

The Community's major home iron ore reserves stretch along the Côtes de Moselle in Lorraine from Nancy to Longwy and on into southern Belgium and Luxembourg. There is also an exploited

58

outlier underneath the Jurassic limestone around Briey. These Liassic 'minette' ores are low grade with a high phosphorus content, and consequently were of little use for making good steel until the invention of the basic process in the 1880s. In the last decade of the

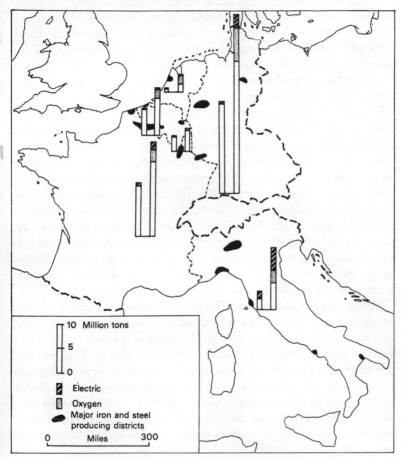

Fig. 11. Steel production by country, 1925 and 1965.

nineteenth century a powerful iron and steel industry based upon them was established in France and Luxembourg, and during the twentieth century this has continued to grow. The main centres in France are Thionville, Hayange, Joeuf and Seremange, and in Luxembourg, Petange and Dudelange. A big problem has been the lack of nearby supplies of good coking coal; that of Lorraine, being of inferior quality, was at first little used. Most of the coal has generally been brought by rail and inland waterway from the Ruhr and Franco-Belgian coalfields. An iron and steel industry has also grown up on the nearby Saar coalfield using Lorraine as well as imported ore.

It can be seen from this that the iron and steel industry is highly concentrated in that area bounded by the Nord, the Ruhr and Lorraine. This has come to be known as the 'Heavy Industrial Triangle' and has for long dominated the steel industries of the northern Community countries. Although by the twentieth century the existence of the Triangle had in the geographical sense become an established fact, economically its unity was far less obvious since it had grown up in an area divided by the frontiers of three nations, frontiers which had been drawn without any regard for the location of natural resources.[2] Each of these three—and later four—parts was therefore within a different economic system, and each came to be more closely associated with other regions in its respective country than with the adjacent parts of the Triangle. An example of this has been the relationship of the Ruhr and Lorraine which logic suggests should be complementary to one another, but whose relations have in fact been less close than one might have supposed. This has in part been caused by technical factors, but it was also due to the separation of the two after 1918 by a political frontier which was rapidly to freeze into an economic one.[3]

It was also *ipso facto* undesirable to have industrial regions too near to the frontiers since this made them both strategically vulnerable and economically peripheral. The Triangle as a whole suffered to a certain degree from these disadvantages in the eyes of national governments, and this was a reason for persistent attempts to obviate too great a dependence on it. The Germans adopted a policy of encouraging industrial development farther east in Saxony and Silesia, while in France the Massif Central, which had little to commend it in the economic sense, was favoured for strategic reasons.[4]

By 1952 the industrial regions within the Triangle were still responsible for some 86 per cent of the steel and 90 per cent of the pig iron produced in the Community. It included the whole output of Luxembourg, and the overwhelming part of that of France, Belgium, and West Germany. Two-thirds of the steel produced outside the Triangle at this time was from Italy, mainly from the Milan-Turin industrial region and from the steelworks at Piombino adjacent to the country's largest reserves of iron ore.

This pattern of steelmaking remained substantially the same until well after the establishment of the Coal and Steel Community.[5] In recent years, however, changes to the economic and technical background to steelmaking have been reflected in the gradual emergence of new centres. One of the most significant developments is a loosening of the bonds which have in the past tied the greater part of the industry so closely to the coalfields. As a result of improved techniques of production, much smaller quantities of coal are now needed in the smelting process, and this has meant that coal transport has become relatively less important in the total cost of steel. In addition, improvements in transport facilities enable the coal to be moved through the interior more cheaply and easily than in the past. The other initial advantage of the coalfields, the black and clay band ores, have long ceased to be of any importance, and even limestone frequently has to be moved considerable distances. Besides this Community coal is becoming increasingly uncompetitive in world markets, and ever larger quantities are being imported into Italy and the Netherlands which have in the past been so handicapped by the lack of indigenous fuel, and also increasingly into the large coal-producing countries themselves (Fig. 13).

Even more revolutionary in its implications has been the introduction of alternative methods of steelmaking, notably electric and oxygen converters, in which coal is not required at all or is needed in far smaller quantities than in conventional methods. A further technical development has been the increasing use of large integrated plant which are able to carry out on one site all the processes from smelting to rolling, so saving on heat and material transfers. Already by 1961 90 per cent of the Community's pig iron, 80 per cent of the crude steel and 66 per cent of rolled products were coming from steelworks of this sort. The coalfield regions do not as a rule provide very suitable sites for such plant, both because of the large amount of industry already in them and because the land surfaces are frequently unsuitable for large structures.

As in the case of coal, home iron ores are increasingly proving inadequate to supply the Community's requirements. These low grade ores are expensive to transport compared with high grade imports, which not only contain less useless material, but can now be brought in cheaply by bulk carrier. Another raw material of increasing significance to the steel industry is scrap, coming both from home and abroad, and the sources of supply of this are unrelated to those of iron ore.

Developments have been further influenced by changes which have taken place in economic, social, and political circumstances. In the past, the principal markets for steel products were the heavy industries which normally clustered in its vicinity and were supplied with a limited range of shapes and qualities of steel. During the present century new metal industries have been springing up away from the old industrial districts, and since the establishment of ECSC this process has been accentuated. The markets for steel products have therefore become more widely distributed and their requirements more varied.

One of the best-known direct consequences of ECSC has been the removal of the frontier tariffs and quotas which impeded international trade in iron and steel. Less dramatic, but of great importance also, has been the obligation on governments to get rid of all forms of subsidy unless they are for particular reasons approved by the High Authority, and one of the most important of these to be removed has been the discrimination in transport rates which used to put foreign competitors at a disadvantage in trying to sell in any of the other five national markets.

The establishment of ECSC has also altered the whole framework in which the iron and steel industries are operating. They are now catering for a market which is many times the size of even the largest of the national ones, and this has changed the optimum conditions of production both geographically and economically, the transformation being most marked around the central frontier zone. The frontiers have now ceased to be barriers, and locations adjacent to them are no longer considered to be either economically or politically undesirable. In fact the whole situation has now been turned inside out, and these areas are now right in the centre of the economic life of the new unit. [6]

The opportunities presented by this new situation can be grasped on the required scale because of the freeing of capital flows and the beginning of intra-Community economic association by mergers and agreements. A further direct influence exerted by the Community is through its regional policy. The steel industry is designed to play a part in this and as a consequence new developments have occurred in areas which on short-term economic grounds would not be particularly attractive. A consideration of the changes which have come about in the geographical pattern of steelmaking in the Community resolves itself into two parts: there are the new developments outside the Triangle and the changes which have been taking place within it.

Outside the Triangle the most important development has been the move to the coasts. Between 1953 and 1963 the output of

ECSC's coastal steelworks increased from 1·3 million tons to 7·1 million tons, so increasing from 3 to 10 per cent of the Community's total. By 1966 the capacity of the eight coastal works in operation was 15·1 million tons, 14 per cent that of the Community. They are located in two groups, each with approximately the same capacity, one along the North Sea coast and the other in southern and

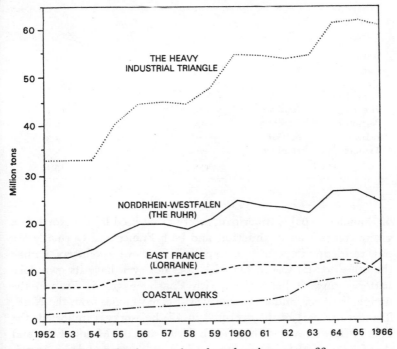

Fig. 12. Steel output by selected regions, 1952–66.

western Italy.[7] Each of the four Italian plants are about the same size, but the northern ones vary considerably, the largest of them being Ijmuiden, the biggest coastal steelworks in the Community, which produces the greater part of the Netherlands' output.

These new plants are all situated in response to the new conditions of production which we have already considered, paramount among which is the increasing need to import raw materials, and they eliminate the cost of transport to the interior which is a disadvantage of the older home-resources based works. The Community's imports of coal from third countries rose from 22 million tons in 1952 to 29 millions in 1965, but over the same period imports of iron ore quadrupled from 13·5 to 53·7 million tons, and already by 1963 all the Community countries had become net importers of both coal and ore. Virtually all the coal used in the Italian works is brought in by sea, the greater part of it from the United States, but although half

Table 11. ECSC—Output of Coastal Integrated Steel Plants, 1953, 1963 and 1966. (Million tons)

Location	Company	1953	Output 1963	1966 (Potential)
Bremen	Klöckner	—	0·94	1·6
Ijmuiden	Hoogovens	0·65	2·03	2·45
Dunkirk	Usinor	—	0·55	1·5
Cornigliano	Italsider	0·1	1·63	2·1
Piombino	Italsider	0·19	1·13	2·1
Bagnoli	Italsider	0·36	0·86	2·0
Zelzate	Sidmar	—	—	1·3
Taranto	Italsider	—	—	2·0
Total		1·3	7·1	15·1

(Source: Fleming, *The Geographical Review*)

of Ijmuiden's coal is American, most of that used by the North Sea group comes from the interior, and both France and Germany are now restricting imports so as to protect their own producers. Unlike the other coastal works, Dunkirk does not even have its own coke batteries since it has agreed with Charbonnages de France, the nationalized coal industry, that it will take supplies from the Nord. The greater part of the ore used in all the works is imported, the bulk of Italy's coming from North Africa and the Middle East, and that for the northern group primarily from Sweden and the American continent.

Table 12. ECSC Trade in Iron Ore and Scrap for Selected Years. (Million tons)

	(Millon tons) 1954	1960	1965
Iron ore from other Community countries	10,956	26,448	20,923
Iron ore from third countries	12,590	34,192	53,717
Scrap from the Community	1,852	3,324	4,954
Scrap from third countries	527	1,708	1,473

(Source: Siderurgica 1964 No. 1 and 1967 No. 1, Statistical Office of the European Community)

When choosing sites, account had to be taken of the availability of plenty of suitable land with nearby deep water for the bulk carriers. Six of the works are capable of being expanded to a capacity of 5 million tons per annum, and all but one have facilities for berthing

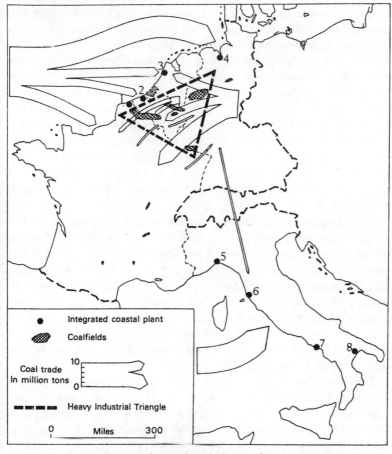

Fig. 13. Integrated coastal steel plant and trade in Coal.
1. Dunkirk 2. Zelzate 3. Ijmuiden 4. Bremen 5. Cornigliano
6. Piombino 7. Bagnoli 8. Taranto

ore carriers of 35,000 tons DWT. The one exception is the Klöckner works at Bremen, which is limited to vessels of 28,000 tons, but this also uses the new supercarrier berths at Weserport.[8]

A further important development with a bearing on this is the increasing consumption of scrap, which between 1954 and 1965 doubled to 36·9 million tons. About a half of this is used by Germany, and Italy follows with nearly a quarter. However, while it is the raw material for about a third of Germany's steel, and about the same proportion of that of France, it is used to make 60 per cent of the Italian output. Over a half of this is imported, the greater part coming by sea from France and Germany. This is a further attraction of the coasts for the Italians, and although it is less so for the northern group they have the further advantage of being situated in the Community's major scrap-surplus region.

The movement away from old centres has also been encouraged by the increasing amounts of oxygen and electric steels for which no coal is required. In 1957 only half a million tons of oxygen steel was made, while by 1965 it had risen to 16·5 million, 20 per cent of the Community's total, and every one of the coastal plants has either LD/Kaldo converters or oxygen lance attachments. All the oxygen steel made in Italy and the Netherlands comes from coastal works, as also does a large part of that of France and Belgium, but Germany does not fit into this pattern and three-quarters of its output comes from the Ruhr.

Since in present conditions it would be quite impossible for the whole output of the Italian coastal plants, and particularly those in the south of the country, to be absorbed locally, their sites make it easy for the products to be taken to the consuming centres by sea. The northern plants have the advantage of being situated near to regions which have been developing rapidly in recent years, and which have large steel-consuming industries in their vicinities. There is no local labour shortage in either, and in any case with the increasing substitution of capital for labour, the attraction of the 'labour pools' has considerably diminished.

The bonds with the old industrial clusters have been further weakened by the growth of new industries distributed over a wide area which require large quantities of rolled steel, coil, piping and wire. The northern coasts are good distribution points for this variety of products, but the Italian coastal sites do not have this sort of advantage since their greatest markets are in the north.

The other major steelmaking region outside the Triangle is in northern Italy where the main centres are Turin, Sesto San Giovanni, Bergamo, and Brescia. This is the old pre-coastal core of Italian steelmaking, akin to the Triangle in the north, but since it lacks coal and iron it has to rely heavily on hydroelectricity and scrap. After the Second World War the Sinigaglia plan advocated the concentration of Italy's iron and steel production into coastal sites, but with its large capital investment and nearby markets, the north has retained its dynamism. The region's capacity in 1965 was 7·5 million tons and two-thirds of it was electrically made.[9]

In spite of all the spectacular developments outside it, the Triangle has remained incontestably the centre of the Community's steel-making, although its relative importance has been declining. In 1952

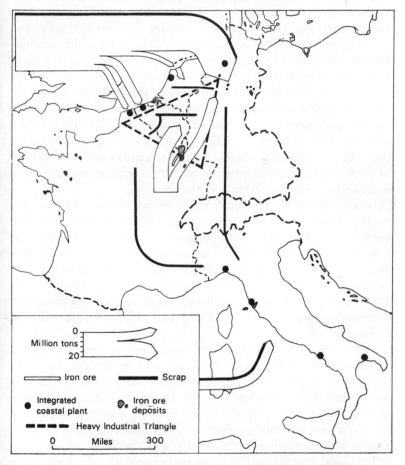

Fig. 14. Integrated coastal steel plant and trade in iron ore and scrap.

with an output of 33·7 million tons it was responsible for 86 per cent of all steel made in the Community, and still higher proportions of the individual national totals in the case of France, Belgium, and Germany. By 1965 the region's output had nearly doubled to 61·4 million tons, which was however only 70 per cent of the Community

67

total. This relative decline was due principally as we have seen to the upsurge in Italian steelmaking together with the 'drift to the coasts'. Still, growth within the Triangle has been considerable, and it has been brought about both by the modernization of existing steelworks and the building of new ones in the same regions. During the six years between 1955 and 1960 70 per cent of new German investment in the steel industry went into the Ruhr alone, and 60 per cent of the French went into Lorraine, thus tending to confirm the existing geographical pattern of the industry.[10] Since 1960 the amounts invested in these areas have in each case declined and a large proportion of subsequent new investment has gone to the coasts. The continuance of a high level of investment in the Triangle is by no means due to what geographers call 'geographical inertia' because the area still possesses immense advantages. Almost all the coking coal and a large proportion of the iron ore and scrap used still come from within it, and the adequate communications network built up to serve these industries together with the large adjacent markets make this a very obvious place for steelmaking.

Besides this the Community's output of coal and iron ore has been tending more and more to concentrate into the Triangle. The only orefield in which output has been increasing is Lorraine, and it is now responsible for 70 per cent of the Community's total. We have already seen how the most healthy coalfields are those in the area extending from the western Ruhr to Lorraine, and this latter has now the added advantage of coking coal of its own, since with modern processes Lorraine coal can at last be used satisfactorily in the blast furnaces.

The proportion of the Triangle's steel coming from the Land of Nordrhein-Westfalen, mainly the Ruhr and its vicinity, increased between 1952 and 1965 from 40 to 44 per cent, and this has been at the expense largely of the Saar and Luxembourg both of which now account for a smaller proportion than formerly. Lorraine's share has also decreased very slightly from 21 to 20 per cent, but that of the Franco-Belgian coalfield has remained quite stable.

The Ruhr benefits both from its coking coal and the good water communications with the North Sea, and since the canalization of the Moselle in 1964 it has had direct water communication with the Lorraine orefield, which remains an important source of Germany's iron ore, although in recent years it has been getting gradually less so. In 1962 9 million tons of it were imported, one-third of the total German imports of ore, but by 1965 imports from this source had fallen to 6 million tons, only one-sixth of the total. By contrast, the imports of high-grade ore, particularly from West Africa and South America, are on the increase.

The greatest importer of Lorraine ore is the BLEU which in 1965 took 15 million tons, supplying two-thirds of its total requirements. Most of this is for Belgium which has practically no home supplies.

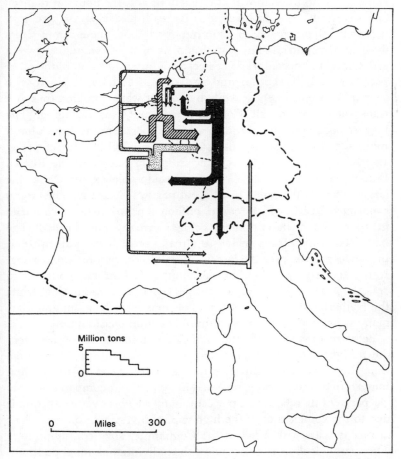

Fig. 15. Intra-Community trade in steel (all types), 1965.

The Moselle canalization has actually been more of a boost for Lorraine than for the Ruhr, since it gives cheap transport for the main supplies of coking coal, and the introduction of single through rail rates for Ruhr coke has meant a saving of 30 per cent in the freight costs. Dependence of Lorraine on Ruhr coking coal remains strong, and still over a half of the supplies come from there. The

69

region's central location in relation to the new large market is a further advantage, and it is now able to supply southern Germany as well as the growing industries of eastern France.

Following the establishment of ECSC there was an immediate increase in the internal trade both in iron ore and in coal, and this coincided with the removal of restrictions and the boom in the iron and steel industry. However, this increase has fallen off and now lags well behind the increases in imports of both these commodities from third countries. The establishment of the Community gave a great boost to internal trade in steel also, but unlike that of the other two, this has been kept up, and rose from 1·8 million tons in 1952 to 11·7 million tons in 1965, while by 1966 it was 13 million tons at a time when the overall Community output was declining. The biggest net importer is France, whose imports sprang from almost nil in 1952 to 454,000 tons in 1954 and 3½ million tons in 1965 (Fig. 15). Almost all her imports came from Germany and the BLEU. France has now also developed a considerable export trade, the largest share of this going to adjacent parts of Germany. The largest exporter is BLEU which sent 3½ million tons to the other countries in 1965, the main customers being Germany and France. The Netherlands and Italy, which as already seen, have built up their industries rapidly over the last two decades, do very little exporting. Italy imported 1·3 million tons from other Community countries in 1965, representing only 10 per cent of her total consumption, while the Netherlands imported 1·7 million tons from Belgium and Germany which was over 50 per cent of her total consumption.

Between 1965 and 1966 the total Community output of steel went down slightly from 86 million tons to 85·1 million tons. At the same time the Community capacity increased from 102 to 105 million tons, so that unused capacity stood at 19 per cent compared to only 7·4 per cent in 1964 and 4 per cent in 1960. This overproduction is due to the coincidence of the high capital investment on new plant in recent years with a fall in the Community steel consumption.[11] The overall decline does not reflect the individual national positions, since in Italy and the Netherlands, with high home demand and small exports, production continued to rise, while in the BLEU and Germany home demand slackened off and exports were adversely affected by the general decrease in consumption. Only in France was output quite stable, a response to the buoyancy of the rest of the country's economy.

Perhaps the greatest single effect which ECSC has had on the steel industry is to have enabled the European steelmakers to calculate with a higher degree of certainty on the permanence of factors which in the past have been ephemeral and liable to sudden changes.

These new circumstances are mirrored in the changing geography of the industry. The Triangle, for so long the hub of the steel industries of France, Germany and Benelux, has now been extended to the adjacent North Sea, and across the Alps the old centre of production in the upper Po has likewise been stretched in an even more spectacular manner to the Italian coasts. The provision of raw material, fuel, capital, and labour are now for the first time being planned on a continental scale, and the new plants are intended in turn to supply a continent-sized market.[12] As N. J. G. Pounds has put it, 'From the geographical point of view the most interesting aspect of the operation of the Common Market for Coal and Steel is that it will assist in locating new plant, not in the best situation for a particular country, but from the point of view of the Community as a whole'.[13]

Nevertheless, even though they might be in the best interests of the Community as a whole, governments are still chary of allowing changes in this vital industry which in their opinion might be prejudicial to national self-sufficiency. In periods of overall prosperity each country has shared in it, but when economic activity stagnates or declines then the more efficient locations are naturally favoured by firms for their production and investment, and it is in such circumstances that the desire for national protection begins to reassert itself. In 1966 the French government brought out a plan for subsidising coking coal, and another in 1967 for the rationalization of the country's steel industry with the aid of a low-interest government loan. It is this kind of thinking along national lines and putting political before economic considerations that tends to slow down the process of adjustment to changed conditions, which in an industry like this one is, in any case, a very slow one.

General Manufacturing

Although manufacturing of various sorts is very widely distributed throughout the Community, and few parts of it are without industries at all, there are certain areas in which there is a high degree of industrial concentration. The most important of these are the Greater Ruhr, the Middle Rhinelands, central Belgium, Randstad Holland, the Paris region, and the Little Triangle of northern Italy. A number of lesser, but still important regions, include Lower Saxony, Mid-Bavaria, the Nord, and the Rhône corridor. Each region has its own particular industrial character, and although the larger ones generally duplicate one another's manufactures, there is nevertheless a discernible tendency to specialization.

The Ruhr is essentially a steel and heavy metallurgical district, but a number of specialized sub-regions have grown up around it which draw on it for power and raw materials and supply manufactured goods to its five million people. To the south are the Wuppertal clothing towns and near them Solingen and Remscheid with their cutlery and special steels. On the other side of the Rhine is the textile region centring on Krefeld, and along the river itself from Duisburg to Cologne is a mixed area specializing in chemicals, synthetics and engineering. Beyond the Lower Rhine Highlands, extending from Frankfurt southward and stretching up the Neckar to Stuttgart, is Germany's other major industrial region, concentrating particularly on transport equipment and general engineering.

The Paris area, with eight million people, is the largest single concentration of population in the whole Community and has a varied industrial structure including motor vehicles, aircraft, electrical engineering, and chemicals, besides the luxury clothing, foodstuffs, and perfumes for which it is renowned the world over. A similar range of manufactured goods is made in the industrial region of Piedmont and Lombardy, centring on Milan and Turin, but northern Italy is also the Community's largest textile manufacturing region, and Genoa is one of the country's two principal shipbuilders, the other being Trieste. In mid-Belgium also there is considerable variety, with textiles, particularly cotton and linen of great importance, also shipbuilding around Antwerp, and chemicals and general engineering around Brussels. The Randstad had a wide range of manufacturing, mostly consumer goods, with a particular specialization in electrical equipment and machinery.

Of the second rank industrial regions, Lower Saxony has the Community's most important shipbuilding centre at Hamburg, and further inland the Wolfsburg-Hanover-Brunswick region is particularly noted for motor vehicles and their components. Bavarian industry centres on Munich and Nuremberg, and here there is a great variety of industries, notably textiles, precision engineering, components, and chemicals. The twin centres of the Rhône corridor are Marseilles and Lyons, respectively the second and third largest cities in France. The former has a great variety of industries in its vicinity, notably shipbuilding, chemicals, food processing, and engineering. The latter is well known for silk manufacture, but has now gathered a number of engineering industries, notably the making of textile and other machinery. The Nord of France has a combination of textiles and heavy engineering similar to that found in adjacent west Belgium, while Lorraine and the Saar, though principally iron and steel areas, have industries manufacturing heavy machinery and engineering products.

It can be seen from this outline that the pattern of general manufacturing in the Community is a very complex one, and it is far from easy to produce all-embracing explanations to account for it. Each industrial district has grown up in response to individual factors which have, in each case, contributed to producing its own particular character. However, it is possible to distinguish two groups of industries, those which grew up in the nineteenth century and those which did not become of importance until the twentieth, and each one of these has developed its own distinctive geography.

The most important industries in the first group are structural engineering, metallurgy, heavy chemicals, locomotives, textiles, and shipbuilding. Like iron and steel these grew up either on or as near as possible to the coalfields from which they drew all their power and much of their raw material. Today, although they have changed their methods, and do not use coal directly, they still remain highly concentrated around the central coalfield belt and its Saar-Lorraine outlier. The shipbuilding industry is obviously a special case, but the greatest production is on the coast stretching from Dunkirk to Hamburg which is the most accessible to receive materials from the heavy industrial areas of the interior, and accounts for about two-thirds of the Community's output.

In the second group the major industries consist of motor vehicles, aircraft, electrical and electronic equipment, machinery—electrical and other—machine tools, man-made fibres, and synthetics. A common characteristic of all of them is that they do not use coal directly since their energy is provided mostly by electricity and, to a lesser extent, gas. This has released them from the beginning from the ties of the coalfields and given them a wide choice of possible locations, but it has not made them 'footloose'. They use a variety of raw and semi-finished materials and need to be well placed to obtain them without incurring excessive transport costs. Besides this they must have good communications with their component and raw material suppliers and their markets, and they must be ensured of an adequate supply of labour.

These industries first grew to importance in the inter-war years, and at the outset large cities, such as national and regional capitals, which had not normally been attractive to the older industries,

73

proved to be ideal situations for them. Their varied industries which could be adapted to supply components, traditionally mobile labour force, and large markets for goods which remained luxuries until well after the Second World War all rendered them into very suitable

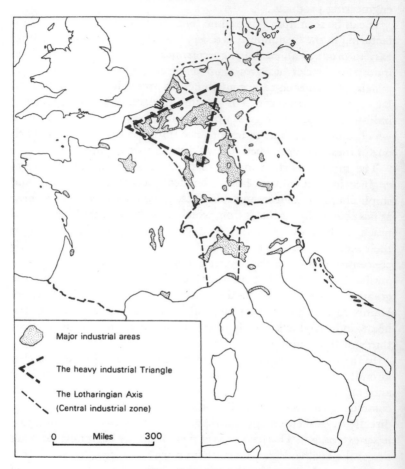

Fig. 16. Industrial regions.

locations. In addition to this such cities usually owed their historic importance to good communications which could now be used to distribute the new products over a wide area. A further requirement was a reasonable proximity to the coalfields which remained an important source of supply for steel and other metals, and in the circumstances the most favoured places were Paris, Cologne, Frankfurt, Stuttgart, Rotterdam, Amsterdam, and Brussels which are all

74

within an economic distance of the coalfields. Smaller scale developments took place in a host of other towns in the German Rhinelands, the Low Countries, and northern Italy.

In the years since the establishment of the Community this industrial pattern has come to be more and more modified by economic, technical, and political developments, many of which had their origins in earlier years but which have only recently come to exert a significant influence on industrial location. There has been an unparalleled expansion of production in the Community countries, which has been particularly spectacular in the newer branches of industry. Increases in output can most effectively be brought about by increasing the size of plant, and this has made the intelligent siting of factories all the more important. At the same time, the transport of raw materials and manufactured goods has become easier and cheaper as a result of technical and other improvements to the communications system. In the political field, the territory of Western Europe has been drastically reorganized by the division of Germany followed by the fusing together of the Six, and this has profoundly changed the shape and nature of the political unit within which the industrialists in this part of Europe are operating.

As one would expect, it is in the expanding industries that the most significant developments have taken place, since increases in output have necessitated the opening of new premises, frequently in quite new localities. We have already seen how the geography of iron, steel and energy has reacted to the new circumstances, and although in general manufacturing the changes have been less clear-cut, they have been quite as remarkable.

The twin keynotes of the process of change have been a dispersal from existing centres accompanied by a tendency to concentrate into certain new ones. Part of the dispersal can be put down to the desirability of re-locating in other parts of the same industrial complex, but more significant is the spread to entirely new areas, and in this it is possible to distinguish the evolution of a Community-sized 'super-core' which is attracting a disproportionate amount of new industrial investment on account of the advantages it offers to the manufacturers.

By way of example one of the most important and rapidly expanding of the Community's industries, motor vehicles, will be examined and the extent to which these locational tendencies can be observed in it will be assessed.

With a production of over 6 million passenger cars and 550,000

75

commercial vehicles in 1966, the Community came second only to the United States. (Table 13). Since the establishment of the Economic Community in 1958 the output of cars has more than doubled, and that of commercial vehicles has gone up by 70 per cent. Over this period there has been a change in the relative shares of the three large countries which manufacture almost all the Community's vehicles. In 1958 West Germany was turning out a half of the total of each type of vehicle, and of the remainder four-fifths came from France alone. By 1966, however, the German share had dropped to 47 per cent of the cars and 40 per cent of the commercial vehicles, while the greatest gainer has been Italy which produced 20 per cent of the cars and 13 per cent of the commercial vehicles, thus doubling its share in each case. The French share of car output, on the other hand, declined, but in commercial vehicles it rose to 44 per cent to make her the Community's largest single manufacturer.

Table 13. Total Output of Vehicles in the Community Countries, 1958 and 1966 with comparative figures for the United States and United Kingdom

| | 1958 | | 1966 | |
	Cars	Commercial Vehicles	Cars	Commercial Vehicles
Germany (FR)	1,306,854	188,402	2,830,050	220,658
France	968,999	158,550	1,785,906	238,646
Italy	369,374	34,174	1,282,418	83,480
Belgium	—	—	169,000	4,700
Netherlands	—	1,554	32,748	7,426
Luxembourg	—	—	—	—
Community Total:	2,645,227	382,680	6,400,122	554,910
United States	4,257,816	877,296	9,335,200	1,802,600
United Kingdom	1,051,548	312,752	1,722,000	455,200

(Source: Society of British Motor Manufacturers and Traders)

The centres of each nation's production are the great city regions which also dominate in other fields of general manufacture. Four-fifths of French car output is from the Paris region, and in Italy an even higher proportion comes from the Milan-Turin area (Fig. 17).[14] Although in West Germany there is a much greater dispersal, the twin centres are in the Middle Rhinelands and Lower Saxony. With the exception of Lower Saxony which, as we shall see later, is a special case, these are the areas in their respective countries which best combine the provision of labour, markets, component makers, distribution facilities, and adequate power. Although they are not, of course, themselves important power producers, they are principal areas of convergence of primary and derived energy (Fig. 8).

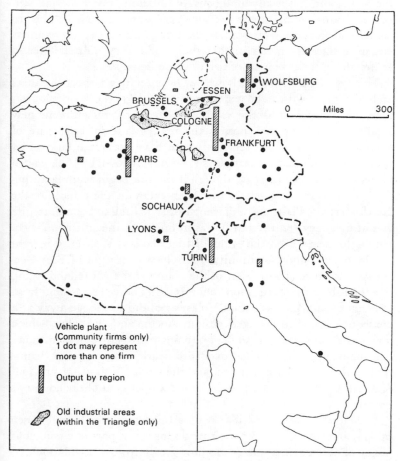

Fig. 17. The motor vehicle industry.

The movement away from congested areas is most clearly seen in the case of the Community's greatest city, Paris. Three of the largest French firms—Renault, Citroen, and Simca—are all in Paris or its vicinity, but the nearest works to the centre is that of Renault at Billancourt, and most of the others are out to the north-west at Nanterre, La Garenne, Clichy, and Asnières. More recently Renault have moved farther to Flins, Rouen, and Le Mans, and Citroen

77

now have a plant at Poissy. This dispersal is motivated by the need for cheap land for building and by the increasing inadequacy of the urban communications to deal with the volume of traffic now using them. The main line of dispersal from Paris is north-westward along the Seine, and this is advantageous for obtaining raw materials and also for distribution to the consumers. Dispersal from the centre has also taken place in other manufacturing cities in the Community, but since they are much smaller than Paris, they do not suffer so acutely from the problems of urban thrombosis.

This type of dispersal is, however, over relatively short distances and takes place within the general orbit of the great city or conurbation. Very different is the establishment of manufacture in new localities which do not possess the ready-made infrastructure of ancilliary industries and services which have made the large cities so attractive. A notable example is Wolfsburg, chosen by Volkswagen for its main factory in 1933, though it did not begin manufacturing there until 1950. Located in the Aller valley in the middle of the North German Plain and adjacent to the Mittelland canal, its site was at first very central and it was in line with the official policy of moving industry from the Ruhr district. Today, Wolfsburg is right on the edge of the Community, literally within sight of East Germany, and since the division of the country, the Mittelland canal, like the Elbe, has lost its importance as a link between east and west. It is significant, however, that Volkswagen did not move away as a consequence of the changed circumstances, and the town, which now has a population of 56,000, remains their centre of operations. Car manufacture has spilled over into nearby Hanover and Brunswick, and even as far as Emden, and the whole 'Volkswagen region' of North Germany now produces about 40 per cent of the country's output.

In south Germany a similar case is Ingolstadt which was chosen in 1932 by Auto Union for their works, again as part of a conscious policy of decentralization. It has now grown from a population of a few thousand to 68,000 and is the largest vehicle-producing town in Bavaria. The firm is now merged with Daimler-Benz whose main centre is at Stuttgart, and Ingolstadt is for them peripheral and has declined relative to the major plants in the Middle Rhinelands, but it remains a very important vehicle manufacturer.

An analogous situation in France is that of the Peugeot factories at Montbéliard and Sochaux in the Jura. This is the only French firm which does not operate principally from Paris, and the choice of these places was largely due to their personal associations for the

founder. The relative success achieved in rather eccentric locations
such as these depends largely on whether the firm is based on them
and conducts its principal operations around them, on how much
of the vehicle the firm actually makes itself, and on how good the communications system is. If, as in the case of Volkswagen and Peugeot,
all these conditions are satisfied, then it is more easily able to overcome the very real disadvantages of a location which is off the
beaten track.

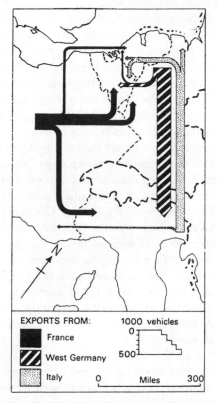

Fig. 18. Intra-Community trade in motor vehicles, 1965.

The coalfields were for a long time largely ignored by vehicle
manufacturers, as indeed they were by most of the other new
industries, although their possession of energy, steel, and labour
supplies are bound to be of some attraction if the great problems of
suitable building land and adequate internal communications can
be solved. As a result of the conscious policy now being pursued of
introducing new industries into the older industrial regions, together

with a very real appreciation on the part of many firms of what these have to offer, this situation is beginning to change. The Ruhr combines the advantages of steel and energy with being a major European crossroads, and in recent years it has lost its exclusively heavy industrial character. In the early 1960s Opel (General Motors) constructed a new works at Bochum, and Krupps now have a commercial vehicle division at Essen. Peugeot, always the odd man out geographically among French firms, have built a similarly sited works near the Nord coalfield at Lille.

Unlike oil refining and iron and steel, vehicle manufacture has not been very attracted to the coasts since it does not use raw materials directly, and since intra-Community trade is at the moment so much more important than are exports to third countries. A significant exception to this is the location of assembly plants set up by firms from outside the Community. Ford and General Motors both have plants at Antwerp and Chrysler one at La Rochelle; out of 18 assembly plants in the Community belonging to British motor firms in 1964, no less than 12 were in the Low Countries, mainly in north Holland and the Brussels-Antwerp area (Fig. 19). Coastal or near coastal sites like this are ideal for the import of component parts, and if well chosen can be good distribution points to a large area of the interior. The popularity of the Low Countries illustrates the significance of their central location which is also seen in the vast hinterlands of their ports. In view of this it is ironic that the home-based vehicle industry of the Low Countries remains small, but this is largely because of the limited home markets and because they are located between what are, after the United States, the world's three largest manufacturing countries. As sites for an industry on a Community scale however, they are not only convenient for imports and for internal markets, but also have a very varied industrial background and a combined population of 22 million.

It is interesting that the distribution of the components factories of British manufacturers is much more related to the Community's motor industry as a whole, with the main concentrations in the Paris area, the middle Rhinelands and northern Italy. Besides this there are new American plants at La Rochelle, Antwerp, and Bochum, and others at Frankfurt, Kaiserlautern, and Strasbourg.

Thus it is possible to see that new investment in the industry is increasingly tending to concentrate in the Rhinelands which is already the most important manufacturing area. It has the most attraction for American investment, but Community manufacturers are also moving in this direction, as with the new Daimler-Benz works at Woerth in the Palatinate, and the Citroen and Peugeot works at Strasbourg and Mulhouse respectively. Of particular importance is the Middle Rhine area from Frankfurt to the Swiss frontier which has the advantage of being very central for an industry which depends on the assembly of a great variety of materials, and the

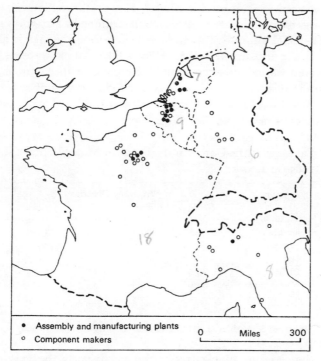

● Assembly and manufacturing plants
○ Component makers
0   Miles   300

Fig. 19. Installations of the British motor industry in the Community.

transport of the product to widely distributed markets.[15] It is also the nearest north European industrial region to Italy which is the recipient of a large part of the intra-Community trade (Fig. 18).

One of the most significant developments for the motor vehicle industry has been the greatly increased intra-Community trade since 1958. In that year only 51,000 vehicles were sold among the six countries, while by 1963 this had grown by over twelve times to 628,000. Of course, over this period all international trade in vehicles increased, but the imports into the Community from third countries went up by only five times. This increasing emphasis on internal trade was clearly related to the lowering of tariffs over this

81

period by between a half and two-thirds, while the tariffs on vehicles entering the Community went up slightly.

Each of the three main producers export large numbers of vehicles, the largest being Germany, which accounts for nearly half the total, followed by France with a further third. The largest importer is BLEU, and this large scale of imports is understandable since it is not itself a significant producer. However, the Netherlands is not a significant producer either, but its imports are only a half those of BLEU although the number of vehicles in service is almost equal; this is because the Netherlands takes larger imports from third countries, notably the United Kingdom with whom she has close trade relations. France imports the smallest number from its partners, with only a third as many as BLEU although she has seven times as many vehicles in service.

Table 14. Intra-Community Trade in Motor Vehicles, 1963 (in 1,000s)

| Importer | Exporting Countries | | | |
	Germany	France	Italy	Total
Germany	—	78·6	78·4	157·0
France	82·8	—	5·7	88·5
Italy	128·4	99·0	—	227·4
BLEU	89·0	99·4	82·6	271·0
Netherlands	82·0	10·6	33·3	125·9
Totals	382·2	287·6	200·0	

(Source: E. Mahler. L'Industrie Automobile. Lausanne 1966)

This increase in vehicle trade, and particularly the very rapid growth of intra-Community trade, is a symptom of the much larger scale on which vehicle manufacturing has now to be planned. In turn this is favouring centrally placed regions, which, besides having the necessary industrial environment, are well placed to distribute to the Community market as a whole. This applies particularly to the Middle Rhinelands area, which is very central to the Lotharingian axis and has unrivalled ease of communication with the rest of the Community.

Conclusion

Industries range from those whose locations are closely determined by a variety of human and physical factors, to those which appear to have very little concern with environment at all.[16] Except for a very few, however, each industry has its own optimum conditions, and this has given rise to the varied pattern of industrial activity throughout the Community. In many cases the original reasons for the siting of a particular industry have ceased to exert any real influence, but, in the absence of new locational pulls, it is unlikely that the industry will move to a totally new area. This 'geographical inertia' is now characteristic of many of the Community's older industries, such as textiles, cutlery, and pottery which are either not expanding very rapidly, or which find that re-siting would not give a return commensurate with the great capital outlay it would entail. It is in those industries which have expanded most rapidly since the establishment of the Community that the greatest locational changes can now be detected, and these are now producing the new industrial geography of the Community. They include some of the more rapidly expanding of the older industries, which have broken away from their coalfield sites, as well as many of the newer ones which have, in any case, always displayed inherently greater mobility.

Among these industries two groups can be distinguished, each of them displaying totally different locational tendencies: those whose attraction has principally been towards their raw materials, and those which are more concerned with proximity to one another and with other general considerations.

The industries attracted to raw materials are most particularly those engaged in the processing of materials which are heavy and still costly to transport overland, and they include iron and steel, the smelting of non-ferrous metals, the generating of electric power, oil refining, and heavy chemical processing. They are dependent to a greater or lesser degree on imports, and in most cases this dependence is increasing. While still highly concentrated around the coalfields, they have also sprung up on coastal, estuarine, and major waterway sites which are good places to handle imports and from which processed materials can be moved easily into the interior. Most important in the north is the stretch of coast from the Seine to the Elbe together with its estuaries and waterways, while in the south the Rhône delta region is of great importance, and in Italy some of the country's most important industries are now found around the northern and western coasts. Frequently also these industries have attracted others such as chemicals and petro-chemicals, gas works, and metallurgical processing all of which need a constant supply of their products or by-products, and together they constitute very distinct industrial complexes.

The second group consists of the secondary manufactures ranging in type from vehicles and kitchen equipment to aircraft and computers. These consist almost entirely of newer industries which have grown to importance in the last half century, and they have gravitated first and foremost to the national core regions which have, as a consequence frequently become the main centres of general industry (Fig. 16). This is because such areas, for a variety of reasons, had the right sort of economic climate in which they could flourish, and the process of concentration has itself added to this by strengthening the industrial infrastructure. Yet this tendency to concentration in its most extreme forms has in many ways been brought about by 'geographical inertia', as has, for example, the continued specialization of Solingen on cutlery and Lyons on silk. This is because it is far simpler from the point of view of the individual industrialist to gravitate to existing industrial groupings than to strike out elsewhere, although it is not necessarily to the advantage of the economy as a whole that this should be done. There are notable examples of industrial decentralization, some intentional and some fortuitous, which have been very successful. The main Volkswagen factory at Wolfsburg became peripheral as a result of political circumstances outside the firm's control, but it remains West Germany's most important vehicle firm; Philips Electricals established their main works at Eindhoven, over 70 kilometres from the main industrial area of the Randstad, while Sud Aviation has developed successfully at Toulouse in an even more peripheral site as a result of conscious policy on the part of this state-owned company.

In the case of the young 'science-based' industries of the Community, such as electronics, telecommunications equipment, computers and nuclear materials, there has been a similar tendency to gravitate towards the economic cores in the absence of positive efforts to decentralize. Some decentralization has been brought about in all the countries, and it would seem that many of these industries are amenable to this more easily than are their more 'bread and butter' counterparts which are more closely tied to specific markets and to one another.

There are therefore two balancing tendencies, one to concentration which is encouraged by the conditions created by the Community, and the other to dispersal which is fostered by the regional policies which both it and the individual states pursue. Both of these tendencies will be examined in greater detail in later chapters.

5 The Responsibilities of Unity: Regional Policy in the Community

Robert Marjolin, formerly vice-president of the Commission, once said that in the Community there are as many regional problems as there are regions. While this is true in the widest sense, it is indisputable that there are certain areas in which the problems are particularly acute, and these are recognized by a combination of such features as high unemployment rates, standards of living well below the Community average, declining industries, low per capita energy consumption and little new private investment. The per capita domestic product in the poorer parts of the Community is as little as a quarter that of the richer ones, and in such areas the per capita energy consumption is frequently under one eighth that of the most highly industrialized.

This disparity between one region and another arises from the natural tendency of industry to concentrate into certain favourable places, and for the rest to decline in consequence. The results of this process have been very much in evidence in each individual country where the economic core regions have had the lion's share of growth. and now the existence of the Community has put the whole thing on to a far larger scale. Broadly speaking, the Community's problem regions are of two sorts, those around the edges and those near the centre, and each has its own characteristic difficulties. Within this generalization it is possible to distinguish five regional groupings, within each of which conditions are broadly similar.

The biggest and most intractable problem areas are Western France and Southern Italy. These areas are both peripheral and remote from the main centres of economic activity, and over the years they have declined in importance with the increased concentration in the Paris and Milan-Turin regions respectively. Their problems are due not only to distance, but also to inadequate transport systems, lack of capital to exploit local resources, and a limited local market due to the low living standards. It is in Southern Italy—the Mezzogiorno—that all these problems are most acute, and Western France does not face problems of anything like the same magnitude.

There are also a number of smaller rural areas, in particular in a belt stretching from the northern Netherlands through Lower Saxony which have fallen behind the nearby industrial areas in investment and standards of living. A problem area of a special sort is the eastern frontier zone of the Federal German Republic extending from Schleswig-Holstein to eastern Bavaria. Since the division of the country there has been a movement of population and economic activity westward leaving a sort of 'cordon sanitaire' along the frontier which it has proved very difficult to revitalize.

While all these areas are part of the 'outer zone' away from the economic heartland, there is another more centrally situated group whose problem is industrial maladjustment. This consists particularly of areas whose basic industries are declining or in need of considerable modernization, notably the French Nord, the Borinage and Liège areas of Belgium and the Saar and Siegerland in Germany. The coalfields of the Massif Central and the Lorraine heavy industrial district also have the same sort of difficulties. In addition there are those areas situated along the internal frontiers of the Community which in the past have been unpopular for political reasons, and which now have to be adapted to a completely changed set of circumstances.

While the stimulation of regional growth is very much a Community responsibility, it is at the national level that the basic regional policies have been worked out. The problem exists in all six countries, but each different government has its own approach to it and uses the instruments which it considers most appropriate in the circumstances. These instruments are fourfold: there is the creation of the necessary infrastructure of communications, power and water supplies, houses and schools. Associated with this is direct state investment in industry so as to provide a 'lead' for other investments. Private finance may be encouraged by grants, tax rebates and low-interest loans, and this can be associated with legislation to prevent further industrial expansion in certain areas and so direct it to others.

In France the 'Aménagement du Territoire' policy dates from 1951, and since then all these methods have been used in an attempt to spread economic growth more evenly over the country. The rapid growth of Paris, and the inability of other French cities to provide effective counter-attractions to it, have made regional planning a top priority. In 1963 the country was divided into 21 new economic regions each of which has its own plan for development. The pull of Paris is being counteracted more specifically by

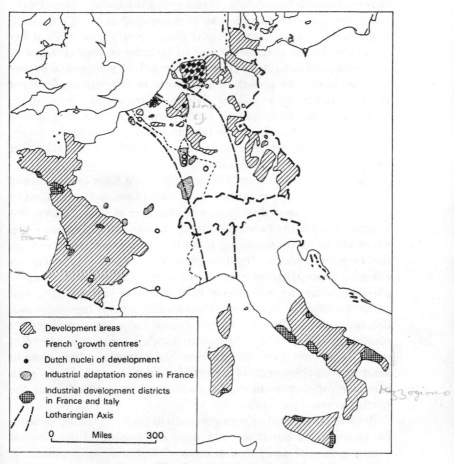

Development areas

o   French 'growth centres'

•   Dutch nuclei of development

Industrial adaptation zones in France

Industrial development districts in France and Italy

Lotharingian Axis

0   Miles   300

Fig. 20. The Development Areas.

the setting up of eight 'growth centres' at Lille/Roubaix-Tourcoing, Nantes/St Nazaire, Bordeaux, Toulouse, Marseilles, Lyons/St Étienne, Nancy/Metz, and Strasbourg. A great deal of public investment is now being concentrated into these places in the hope of stimulating regional growth around them. In addition to this, grants, loans and tax rebates are being given to industrialists establishing factories away from the 'Grande Couronne' around Paris, and especially high inducements are being given to industry in Brittany, Western Normandy, Aquitaine and the south of the Massif Central.

In Italy the attention of the planners and economists has long been directed towards the problem of redressing the balance between the north and the south, and it was to this end that the 'Cassa per il Mezzogiorno' was set up in 1951. Since then £2,100 million has been spent by the government and its agencies on improvements to the region, and in 1957 the Industrial Areas Law gave special powers for stimulating the growth of a number of selected development zones, in particular at Naples, Salerno, Taranto, and Bari. It has been made the rule that all state companies have to devote a minimum of 60 per cent of their new investment to the Mezzogiorno, and there are tax exemptions, low interest loans, and special grants for firms prepared to move there.[1]

Unlike France and Italy, Germany does not have to take care of a huge and relatively homogenous underdeveloped region. The eastern frontier zone does have some features of such an area, but conditions within it vary from highly industrialized Brunswick and Salzgitter to the unpromising Böhmerwald of eastern Bavaria. In the German Federal Republic it is less easy to implement an effective regional policy than in the other Community countries, partly because the state sector in industry is less powerful, and partly because the lände have considerable powers over their own domestic affairs. However 'central points' have been scheduled for special development, and rail goods tariffs have been equalized in order to help certain regions. Besides this, grants have been given to assist the development of Schleswig-Holstein, and there is an extensive programme of drainage and land reclamation along the north German coastlands.

Regional planning has been government policy in the Netherlands for many years, but it was not until the passing of the physical planning law of 1963 that it secured comprehensive powers to implement it. The aim is to plan the growth of the country as a whole, and to use special means to ensure the balanced development of those areas outside the Randstad. To this end the north of the country, consisting mainly of Friesland, Groningen, and Drenthe, a stretch of the south-eastern area near the German and Belgian frontiers and the whole of the province of Zeeland have been designated as 'Problem Areas', and eighteen development centres— fifteen of them in the north—are getting large state aid for improving transport, education, and the public utilities.[2]

In Belgium the first 'Development Areas' were created in 1959, but in 1966 they were replaced by much larger ones which include most of the southern coalfields, almost the whole of Kempenland, West Flanders and numerous smaller districts including one in the extreme south-east of the country adjacent to the Luxembourg and French frontiers. They cover 23 per cent of the country's total area and 36 per cent of its population, and very attractive financial inducements including grants, loans and tax exemptions are being offered to firms settling in them.[3]

Just as it is the rôle of the national governments to draw up plans which are implemented at regional level, so the emerging rôle of the Community authorities is to coordinate the national schemes, and suggest the most fruitful courses of action in the interests of the Community as a whole.[4] It has become the practice for a committee of planners representative of each country to meet in Brussels for the purpose of coordinating the national schemes, drawing up blueprints for the development of areas of special difficulty, and relating their own efforts to the requirements of individual sectors of the economy. Surveys have already been made of the Luxembourg-Lorraine area and of the Mezzogiorno, and transport plans have been coordinated so that these make the maximum contribution to overall economic integration. The Commission also oversees the individual regional plans, making sure that the areas receiving special treatment do, in fact, merit it and that this is not just a concealed subsidy to industry.

Although the Community does not have the mandatory powers of the national governments, nevertheless it has a number of methods of influencing the course of events. As early as Article 2 the Treaty of Rome states its intention to 'promote throughout the Community a harmonious development of economic activities', and later on it specifies that this is to be brought about by 'reducing the differences existing between the various regions, and by mitigating the backwardness of the less favoured'. The practical manifestations of this policy are the European Investment Bank and the Social Fund, and it is through their activities, and similar ones being conducted by the Coal and Steel Community, that the greatest practical impact has been made.

Under the Treaty the EIB is obliged to give loans for enterprises in the less developed regions, for modernizing and converting old factories and for projects of common interest to a number of member states.[5] It is intended to provide money in cases where this is difficult on the free market, either on account of the type of enterprise or the area in which it is located, and it is hoped that this 'priming the pump' will encourage private investment also. Between 1958 and 1965 the Bank made ninety-five loans within the Community, worth $519 million, and seventy-four of these, making up three-quarters of the money lent, were to Italy.[6] The greatest number of projects aided are in the Mezzogiorno, particularly in the Naples area, eastern Sicily, and parts of Sardinia, and there are far fewer in the 'deep south' of Apulia, Calabria, and Basilicata. The largest loans have gone to the Bagnoli steelworks at Naples, the Taranto steelworks, a monosodium glutamate factory in Apulia, a crepe paper factory in Benevento, and a synthetic fibre plant at Castellaccio di Paliano in Latium. One of the largest loans to Sicily has gone to the irrigation and modernization of the farming at Ogliastro in order to increase its potential for specialized fruit growing. The bank also makes loans for public utilities, such as one for modernizing and enlarging of the Sardinian telephone system and another for doubling the railway track between Eccelente and Rosarno in the toe of Italy. In the north of the country a large percentage of the loaned capital has been for the improvement of trans-Alpine communications such as the Mont Blanc Tunnel, the Brenner motorway and the modernization of the Chambéry-Modane-Genoa railway line (See page 22).

The other main beneficiary is western and southern France which has received over a half of the remaining capital loaned. The largest projects here are irrigation works in Provence, a hydroelectric station on the Lower Rhône, a power station in Brittany and agricultural modernization in Aquitaine.

The other big source of funds for industrial development is the Coal and Steel Authority, and to the end of 1965 this had part-financed eleven projects with a total outlay of $30 million. This is both on a much smaller scale than the activities of the EIB and has a different geographical distribution (Fig. 21). With the exception of one, all the loans are to projects either in or near to old coal or iron regions where unemployment has resulted from running down or rationalization. Of particular importance has been the aid granted to help industrial diversification in Liège, the Borinage and the Massif Central, but by far the largest amount of money, making up a half of the total funds lent, was for works in connection with the Sulcis coalfield in Sardinia. A power station has been built there which will eventually take all the coal produced in the area, and which will supply electricity to the Italian national grid via Corsica.[7] The Coal and Steel Community also operates its own industrial retraining scheme and makes redundancy and removal payments.

It has also agreed to give up to 25 per cent loans to firms wishing to establish in the new Belgian Development Areas, and guarantees other loans which will benefit the old industrial areas.

Many EIB loans have been for agricultural improvement, but this

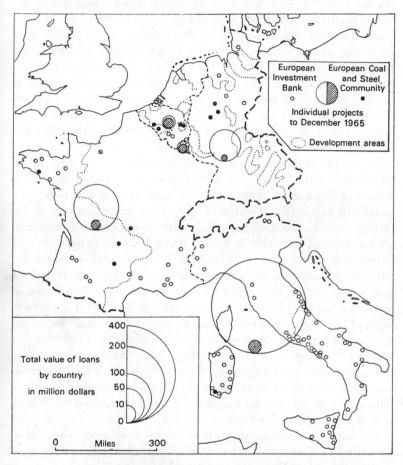

Fig. 21. Projects financed by the Community.

is now the responsibility of the European Agricultural Guidance and Guarantee Fund (EAGGF) which has earmarked $672 million for this purpose between 1966 and 1969. While grants have been made widely throughout the Community, the south of Italy and western France have again been particular beneficiaries (See Chapter 6).

It is quite plain that the places into which the greatest Community investment has gone correspond roughly with the development areas scheduled by the national governments (Fig. 20), and the one major exception to this is the Alpine and sub-Alpine region of France and Italy. Until quite recently south-eastern France was known to some geographers as the 'disinherited corner', but during the last twenty years it has been transformed and is now one of the fastest expanding parts of the country. There is, however, still the need to attract considerable long-term capital for the building of irrigation, hydroelectric and transport undertakings, and the same applies on the Italian side of the Alps. The Community is particularly interested in improving trans-Alpine communications, both because they are of interest to a number of Community countries and thus come within the special terms of reference of the EIB, and also because of the pressing need to link Italy more effectively with the northern member countries.

Of all the problem areas the Mezzogiorno is the one whose difficulties are the most severe and in which the most has been done to try to effect a cure. It covers two-fifths of the country's area, and in 1966 its population of just over 19 millions was 36 per cent of the Italian total. Its isolation from the mainstream of Italian economic life has resulted basically from remoteness from the main centre of industrial activity—it is 1,000 km from Taranto to Milan—from the difficult mountainous terrain and the very poor communications system. Before the unification of Italy in the 1860s it had many industries, but with the establishment of an Italian free trade area it suffered increasingly from northern competition and began to decline. This resulted in the closing down of much of the industry and that drifting away of population to the north and overseas which was to become a flood by the twentieth century. During the Fascist period some attempts were made to modernize communications and improve farmland, but by the end of the Second World War the region remained very backward.

The Italian 'economic miracle' of the postwar years was closely associated with her decision to join the Community. At first this was principally of benefit to the north and widened the gap in living standards between the two parts of the country. In 1951 the average net income per head in the Mezzogiorno was 63 per cent of that in central and northern Italy, but by 1960 it had dropped to only 54 per cent. At the same time unemployment in the north steadily declined from 1948–62, while that of the Mezzogiorno increased after the middle 1950s. It is this situation which has impelled the Italian government since 1951 to spend £2,100 million on a host of measures ranging from the construction of roads to the establishment of new industries. One of the most important measures has been the building of the Autostrada del Sole southward to Naples and then on to Reggio, and while the government's policy is to let tolls pay for the country's motorway network as a whole, it is intended that south of Naples no charges will be made. Other transport improvements are the modernization of the Naples-Reggio railway and the planned continuation of the Apennine line from Terni through Sulmona to Caserta, and special low freight tariffs are in operation throughout the region (See Chapter 2).

Besides this, the state companies have been moving in, and large-scale investment has produced Italsider's Taranto steel works, which is now the largest in Italy, ENI's petro-chemical plants at Ferrandina in Basilicata and Gela in Sicily and Breda mechanical engineering at Bari. There has also been much private investment encouraged by the EIB loans and government tax rebates, notable among them being the Montecatini-Shell petro-chemical works at Brindisi. The siting of two of Italy's nuclear power stations at Latina and Garigliano between Rome and Naples is intended both to provide the region with electric power and also to act as an economic stimulus, and a nuclear fuel processing plant has also been built at Rotondella.

By the early 1960s, however, it was seen that all the effort was failing to produce very fast results and that the gap with the north was not closing. Out of this came the 'development pole' idea canvassed by Emanuele Tosco, the chief economist to Italconsult, Italy's state-owned firm of consultants. This is quite simply an effort to channel as much investment as possible into those areas having the best prospects of benefiting from it so as to create centres of attraction able to withstand competition from outside. In 1962 the Commission ordered a study of the Bari-Taranto area with a view to the creation of a development pole there and this study was completed in 1965. It was found that the industries so far attracted to the area had failed to make a significant impact because they have a very low 'multiplier effect', that is to say they have limited production processes and not particularly close associations with other firms. What is needed, said the report, is a group of interrelated 'multiple cycle' industries to be established together and grow up in mutual dependence. Professor Tosco devised an elaborate technique based on input-output analysis to sift a wide range of mechanical engineering and identify the smallest number of industries with overlapping input requirements that might be able to operate in southern Italy on a fully competitive European basis. This is acting upon the observation that it is closeness to auxiliaries rather than to markets and basic suppliers which is now of greatest importance, and it is essential that industrial growth takes place simultaneously if it is to be effective.[8]

On the basis of this report the Commission put forward a scheme for the creation of a Bari-Taranto development pole and having been

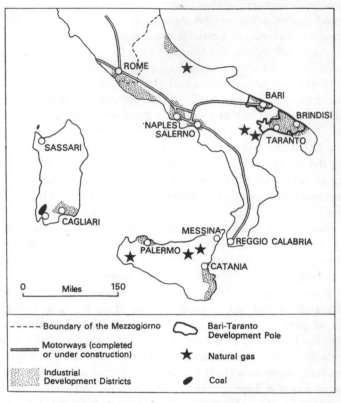

Fig. 22. Developments in Southern Italy.

authorized by the Italian government, work on it began in 1967. Nine main industries and thirty auxiliary ones are being set up and they have all been chosen carefully both to produce an integrated industrial structure and to encourage further investment. The firms are private ones coming from all over the Community, and they have only agreed to move in on the understanding that the others are moving there too. The main manufactures are pumps, excavators, machine tools, cranes, agricultural machinery, structural steelwork, elevators, and domestic appliances, and it is intended that the industrial complex should be a going concern by 1969.[9]

94

The gap between the north and the south of Italy is still a yawning one, but the efforts of recent years are now beginning to pay off. By 1960 hunger had been practically eliminated, and the average income had reached £110 per head per annum, while by 1965 the average income was up to £180 per head. Between 1959 and 1964 industrial investment in the Mezzogiorno grew by 74·7 per cent

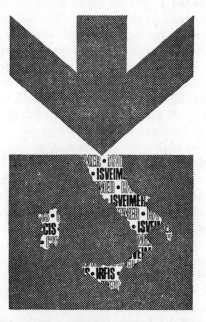

INVEST IN SOUTHERN ITALY

The finance corporations of Southern Italy and the IASM — the official organization for technical assistance in the Italian Mezzogiorno - cordially invite you to visit the **Invest in Southern Italy** office which has been set up in Hall S2 of the « International Trade Centre » at the 45th Milan Fair with a view to providing prospective investors and interested businessmen with detailed information about the numerous possibilities, the unique incentives and far-reaching benefits to be had by investing in Southern Italy.

■ ISVEIMER - Institute for the Economic Development of South Italy's Mainland, Via S. Giacomo 19, NAPLES - Tel. 31.54.75 - Via Meravigli 12, MILAN - Tel. 87.51.83 ■ IRFIS - Institute for the Financing of Industry in Sicily, Via Generale Magliocco 1, PALERMO - Tel. 21.56.74 - Via Broletto 44, MILAN - Tel. 87.47.22 ■ CIS - Sardinian Industrial Finance Corporation, Corso Vittorio Emanuele 68, CAGLIARI - Tel. 56.371 - Via Camperio 3, MILAN - Tel. 80.08.10 ■ IASM - Institute for Assistance to the Development of Southern Italy, Viale Maresciallo Pilsudski 124, ROME - Tel. 80.52.41

Fig. 23. Selling the regions: The Mezzogiorno

compared with a growth rate of 17·6 per cent in central and northern Italy. The important thing now is that the region should gain the capacity for self-perpetuating industrial growth, without the use of artificial stimuli and protection, and the Bari-Taranto project is designed to do this.

The upsurge of economic activity, both here and in the other problem areas, is reflected in their consumption of energy (Fig. 24). The increases in electrical energy consumption have been among the largest in the Community, the most spectacular of all being that of Sicily where between 1953 and 1964 there was an increase of 550 per cent. Similarly there have been very large increases in Apulia (400 per cent) and Basilicata (300 per cent), but Calabria has not conformed to this pattern and the increase there was only 40 per cent. In the whole of France the largest increase over this period was that of Aquitaine which increased by over 300 per cent and likewise large increases were made in Brittany and other parts of Western France, and in the northern Netherlands the rise has also been substantial. These all contrast with the situation in the central problem areas of the Community, where in all cases the increases in consumption have been much smaller.

However, in spite of this, the actual consumption per capita of the peripheral problem areas remains in general the lowest in the Community. In 1964 Calabria, Basilicata and Abruzzi had an average consumption of below 500 kw hours per inhabitant, compared with 3,700 in Nordrhein-Westfalen and over 5,000 in Luxembourg, the highest of all (Fig. 10). On the other hand much of southwest France has a relatively high per capita consumption, as also have the northern Netherlands and adjacent parts of Germany.

Regional development is not all a matter of 'give' on the part of the authorities and 'take' on the part of the regions, since these latter often have a great deal to offer. The release of industry from the pull of the coalfields has enabled it to utilize the advantages of other areas whose lack of power had previously condemned them to a position of secondary importance. One such advantage is the availability of ample cheap space for building factories, roads, houses, schools and all the other things which a community needs. *i.e. exploitation* The labour situation is also likely to be more favourable, and besides lower rates of pay, there is a large labour force which in the case of the Mezzogiorno is increasing by 100,000 each year. The same can also be said of Brittany, Groningen and other parts of the Community where the unemployment rates are now high.

Many of these regions also possess significant natural resources which to a large extent have been exploited only in recent years. Southern Italy has large reserves of natural gas and petroleum which, besides making a significant contribution to the energy supplies, are of value to the petro-chemical industry. Sicily has large reserves of potassium salts which are of particular value in an

96

area where there is such need of fertilizer. South-west France also has petroleum and natural gas, and the northern Netherlands has been found to possess some of the largest reserves of natural gas known to exist. Adjacent to these, in Lower Saxony, are the Community's most productive petroleum fields.

Another important determinant of the prospects of any region is its relationship to others and the long-term significance of this. Fundamental to the difficulties which many of the worst affected problem areas face is the fact that they are peripheral to the main centres of economic activity within the Community. While this is more true of the Mezzogiorno than of anywhere else, the area is, on the other hand, a natural 'land bridge' to the countries of North Africa and it is particularly well located to obtain the oil, natural gas and iron ore which they export to the Community.[10] The new industries of southern Italy are also convenient for markets in North Africa and other parts of the Mediterranean, and manufactures such as pipes and structural steels are being exported in ever larger quantities. With the increased Community imports of coal and iron ore for its steel industries the coastal works of southern Italy are more favourably located than are the interior ones of the north in regard to the supply of raw materials. Increased trade with northern and eastern Europe could likewise transform geographical values in the north of the Community, and convert now unpromising peripheral locations into much more central ones.

It has often been said that the overall effect of the Community will be to increase the disparity between one region and another by making the rich ones richer and the poor ones poorer. Indeed it is true that in the natural conditions of the market inequalities between regions tend to increase rather than to decrease, and this produces what Maurice le Lannou has called 'les monstres urbains, les désertifications, les surpeuplements, les abandons et les friches'*,[11] which have been a feature of industrial states throughout the world. The establishment of the Community has brought this problem for the first time on to a continental scale, since new investment is most attracted to the central parts, so, in the absence of special measures to counteract it, increasing the advantages which they possess over the 'disinherited areas'. Given completely free conditions the disparities in growth could be so great that these latter might actually be retarded by the existence of the Community.[12]

It is in answer to this situation that the Community and national authorities have themselves entered the lists as factors influencing

(*) Urban monsters, man-made deserts, overpopulation, abandoned and waste land.

location and are endeavouring to plan the economic geography and recolonize those areas which have been left behind. The most difficult task is to strike the right balance between the normal play of market forces and the need to ensure a balanced growth throughout

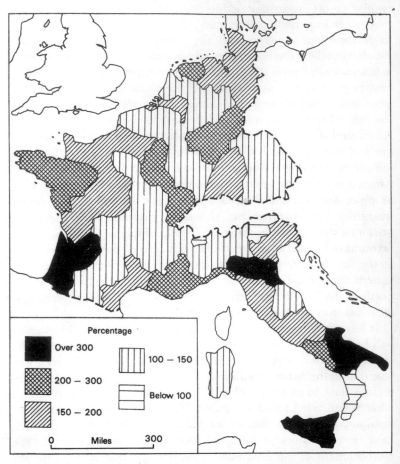

Fig. 24. Increases in electricity consumption by region, 1953–64.

the Community. It is far from being the intention that the large areas which are now getting special privileges should be the permanent patients of a sort of Community health service, but rather that through the use of selected inducements their economic life can be stimulated and they can become quite competitive on their own.[13]

Whilst recognizing the tremendous contribution which positive planning has made to changing the situation, it must be realized that many other factors have also been at work. These include the natural tendency of industry at a certain stage to decentralize, and today this is made more feasible by the improved communications and the mobility of power supplies. Excessive concentration can add to costs and to overall problems, and, to a limited extent, firms counteract this by moving out to new areas of their own accord.[14] There is also the discovery and exploitation of new natural resources and the increased use of known ones, all of which can make formerly unattractive places into very suitable ones almost overnight. Finally, there is the general increase in living standards throughout the Community which is having its repercussions even in the poorest areas and so making them better markets for consumer goods.

The Community planning policies have had the effect of increasing the man-made attractions of the most underprivileged areas, and acting as a catalyst to stimulate their economic activity. In this way it is endeavouring to guide, plan, and increase decentralization and, what is most important, to lead industry into those areas into which it would not otherwise have gone.

6 Food and Agriculture

In the early days of the Six agriculture was one of the principal candidates for unification, but it soon became evident that the establishment of a 'Green Pool' presented problems of unusual magnitude which could not be solved overnight.[1] Later on agriculture was included in the provisions of the Treaty of Rome, but it was not until 1962 that the European Agricultural Guidance and Guarantee Fund (EAGGF) was set up to implement the agreed Common Agricultural Policy (CAP), and since then the Community has become more and more influential in the process of agricultural change.[2] In 1967 final agreement was reached on the financing of the common policy, and on the coming into force of unrestricted intra-Community trade in all foodstuffs.

Agriculture is an activity of considerable economic importance in the Community, and of the total area of 1·17 million square kilometres, 61·3 per cent is classed as being agricultural land. However, the relative importance of agriculture varies considerably between one nation and another. In the Community as a whole it accounts for only 8·2 per cent of the Gross Domestic Product, but while in heavily industrialized Germany it accounts for only 5 per cent, in (until recently) under-industrialized Italy the proportion is 13·4 per cent. Of the others, Belgium is nearest to the German position, and France nearest to the Italian, while the Netherlands is about half-way between the two. The proportion of agricultural land is highest in Italy, occupying two-thirds of the surface, and in the Netherlands it takes up almost as much. At the other end of the scale, in Belgium and Luxembourg the proportion is only just over a half.

Looking still closer, the predominant type of farming also varies very much from country to country within the Community. Of the total agricultural land, just under two-thirds is arable and the remainder pasture. Italy has the highest proportion of agricultural land in arable cultivation, almost three-quarters of the total, while in contrast to this the Netherlands has well over half the land under pasture, and the proportion is similarly high in the other Benelux countries.

In both France and Germany the ratio is about 60 : 40 in favour of arable but owing to the size of the country the actual amount of arable land in France is over double that in Germany. A quarter of the arable land in France is under wheat, and all other cereals together take up another quarter. Although the total size of the arable farmland in Italy is less than two-thirds that of France, the areas producing wheat and maize are in both cases nearly as great, and wheat on its own takes up two-thirds of Italy's cereal acreage.

In both the Netherlands and Belgium over a half of the arable is in cereal production, and while in both countries wheat is the most important cereal, it does not have the dominance which it has in Italy, since barley, oats and rye are also widely grown. Root crops, for fodder and for human consumption, take up a large area, as also does commercial vegetable production. In Germany wheat takes up only a quarter of the cereal lands, less than in any other of the Six, and rye and barley are of almost equal importance to it. The country is also notable for having nine-tenths of the Community rye acreage and half that of potatoes, but green fodder is of much less significance than elsewhere.

Again while Germany has well over a quarter of her total area under woodland, France has only one-fifth, but while in France this is 12 million hectares, in Germany it is only 7 million. In the other countries the amounts of woodland, both actual and proportionate, are much smaller, but they vary from one-sixth of the total land in Italy to only one-twentieth in the Netherlands.

France and Italy together have about 98 per cent of the Community's fruit producing land, but Italy's is by far the larger share because of her greater area in olives and citrus fruit. Together these take up one million hectares, compared to 40,000 in France which is the Community's only other producer of either. The two countries also have an almost equal area under vineyards, but France has four times as much land under beet and potatoes as has Italy.

This overall picture of the main features of the national agricultures, while pointing to the diversity of priorities from country to country, still does not reveal the very real differences existing between area and area within the individual countries. Thus the intensive pastoral and arable farming of the Po valley has very little in common with the extensive sheep and goat rearing of the Apennines and Sardinia, and the French section of the middle Rhinelands has far more in common with adjacent parts of Germany than it has with, say, Normandy or Brittany. Conversely, the agriculture characteristic of north-eastern France extends without interruption into northern Belgium, and from there, with some modifications, through the Börde zone of Germany.

Table 15. Pattern of Land Utilization—1965

| Country | Agricultural area | | Arable land* | Permanent meadows and pastures |
	'000 ha	% of total area	% of agricultural area	
Germany (FR)	13,871	55·8	58·7	41·3
France	33,818	61·3	60·2	39·8
Italy	19,569	65·0	74·2	25·8
Netherlands	2,270	62·9	43·7	56·3
Belgium	1,658	54·3	56·0	44·0
Luxembourg	135	52·2	52·3	47·7
Community	71,320	60·9	63·1	36·9

* Incl. land under permanent cultivation (orchards, vineyards etc.)
(Source: Statistical Office of the European Community)

By piecing together similar areas in different countries, it is thus possible to construct agricultural regions on a Community scale, owing their characteristics to physical and economic considerations of a general character, and in the delimitation of which national frontiers are of secondary importance. The main physical factors involved are climate, soils, and land surface, and while the first determines the broad outlines of the agriculture, the two latter are in large measure responsible for the local details.

There are two principal climatic regions in the Community, the cool temperate maritime of the north and the warm temperate maritime (or Mediterranean) of the south. The cool temperate, with its warm summers, mild winters and all the year round rainfall, is most characteristically developed on the northern and western coastlands, and as one moves into the interior, conditions become steadily more continental, with more extreme temperatures, lower rainfall, heavier winter snow, and a shorter growing season. The Mediterranean, while having warmer overall conditions, is most notable for its very high sunshine totals and lack of appreciable summer rainfall. In its purest form it is confined to the coasts, and towards the interior, continental conditions are found, similar to those north of the central mountain divide.

The change in climatic conditions from north-west to south-east has orientated the agricultural belts in broadly the same direction.

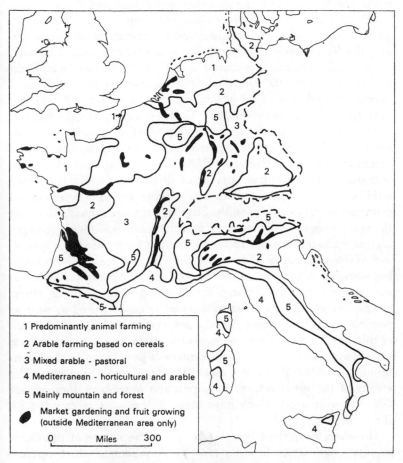

1 Predominantly animal farming

2 Arable farming based on cereals

3 Mixed arable - pastoral

4 Mediterranean - horticultural and arable

5 Mainly mountain and forest

● Market gardening and fruit growing (outside Mediterranean area only)

0   Miles   300

Fig. 25. Major agricultural regions.

Pastoral farming is predominant on the northern and western coasts, while further into the interior arable farming based on cereals and sugar beet becomes the rule, and further in again this changes to mixed farming (Fig. 25). Along the Mediterranean coastlands intensive horticulture and fruit growing is most characteristic, and the adjacent interiors, when they are suitable for farming at all, are in cereal production and cattle and sheep rearing.

However, the final determinant of the quality of the farming practised in any area is the nature of its soils and its relief. For example, the intensive horticulture of South Holland, specializing as it does in bulb-growing and market gardening, has only been made possible by the large stretches of flat land and the rich soils which have developed on the deltaic sediments of the river Rhine. This contrasts with the relatively poor agriculture of Groningen and the Veluwe with their indifferent and sandy soils. Similarly, while arable farming is practised across the North European Plain all the way from the Garonne to Schleswig-Holstein, it is most productive and specialized in a belt stretching from the Paris basin through central Belgium and the Cologne bay to Middle Saxony. Here the combination of undulating relief and good drainage coincides with the largest deposits of fine loess soils. Local relief conditions also themselves contribute to producing valuable micro-climates, and the central uplands of Brittany accentuate the very mild winters of the adjacent coasts without which the growing of primeurs would not be possible. Similarly the south-facing slopes of the scarplands of eastern France and the Rhinelands have the very highest insolation totals which are essential for growing the vine.

Suitable physical conditions will only be used for specialist farming when there is a market for the produce, and while certain foods can be transported great distances and stored for long periods, others are preferably consumed fresh and need to be produced as near as possible to the consumers. Vegetables, certain fruits, and milk are of this type, and they are consequently produced in the immediate vicinities of almost all the great centres of population in the Community, notably Paris, Randstad Holland, and the Ruhr. The effects of the great centres of population have been increasingly felt over wide areas which have come to specialize in catering for their needs.

However, in spite of the way in which the nature of the Community's agriculture is influenced by these factors which operate differentially throughout its area, the precise state of the agriculture in any place depends upon the overall technical and economic level of the particular country and the quality of nutrition which its people are able to afford. It will also be influenced by national economic policies and by the significance of agriculture to the economy as a whole. Thus the Netherlands policy has been to encourage the modernization and specialization of the country's farms, and the resources of a relatively wealthy and technically sophisticated country have thus been employed to establish it as one

of Europe's great farm nations. In contrast to this, until recent years
Italy was backward industrially and had low standards of living,
and this has been reflected in the low levels of agricultural production, particularly in the south of the country. That a high level of
farming does not, however, automatically follow from a high degree
of industralization can been seen from the relative backwardness of
many sectors of German agriculture. This derives from a number of
causes, in particular the concentration of capital investment in
industry, the drift from the land and the rapid rise in the urban
population whose needs could in the first instance most easily be
met by large scale food imports. More recently the situation has
been aggravated by the division of the country which has resulted
in the separation of the industralized west from the agrarian east
which up to then had supplied it with a good part of its grain and
vegetables.

In France, which has nearly a half of the Community's agricultural area, the export to all parts of the world of certain high value
and luxury goods such as wine, meat products, and cheese has
created considerable specialization in certain parts of the country,
but this contrasts with the much more primitive mixed farming
which is still characteristic of large areas.

It is possible to simplify this mosaic of agricultural conditions by
looking exclusively at profitability, and so providing a general guide
to the distribution of high quality farming in the Community.
Employing the criteria devised by S. van Valkenburg*,[3] one can
distinguish a major area of relatively high production extending
across the northern plain from the Gironde to Schleswig-Holstein,
where the overall combination of relief and soil conditions, together
with large markets and relatively advanced techniques are generally
favourable for it. To the south-east of this area is another belt
stretching from Aquitaine through the Massif Central to the
Mittelgebirge where the level of the farming is much lower because
of a less favourable set of physical and human conditions. This is,
however, deeply penetrated by areas of good quality farming, mostly
following the great river valleys, notably the Garonne, Rhône,
Moselle, Rhine, and Main where it has been encouraged by the
better soils and more protected climate.

In the central mountain divide, agriculture, although occasionally
specialized, is generally very sporadic, but to the south of it the

(*) The high production areas were considered as being those with an average
production value of more than $300 per hectare of arable land, a milk production
per cow of not below 2,000 litres, and various other criteria for special crops.

most unique feature is the rapid transition from very intensive cultivation to an almost total lack of any effective farming. This is largely a consequence of the nature of the Mediterranean lands, with their narrow crowded coastal plains backed by high empty plateaux and mountains. The main exception to this is the Po valley which is in many ways an outlier of the North European Plain, although as a result of its climate it is able to sustain a more varied agriculture.

This great variety of types and levels of farming has presented great problems to the Common Agricultural Policy, the aim of which is to raise the general level of the farming and at the same time to establish a single market for its products. These two aspects of CAP are, however, inextricably bound together, since a true agricultural merger has to be paralleled by a rising of the general standards if free trade is not merely to exacerbate the situation. In addition to this, varying yields, weather hazards and overproduction are permanent difficulties for which the common policy has to make provision.

One of the greatest problems which faced the agriculture of the Six was that of low yields. In 1950 the highest wheat yield in the Community—that of the Netherlands—was over 32,000 kg per hectare, and it was nearly as high in Belgium, but those of France and Italy only a little more than half as much, and the German average not much over three-quarters. In barley the Italian yield was only one-third and the French a half of the Netherlands, and the Italian yields of vegetables, sugar beet and fodder were all much lower than those of the same crops in any of the Benelux countries. Those of France were generally nearer to the Italian level, and in the case of maize, and rice actually below it. German yields were almost half as high again as the French in cereals and fodder crops, and quite considerably higher in sugar beet and vegetables.

This very uneven situation was a reflection of the varied levels of mechanization, cooperation and use of fertilizers in the Community. In 1950 Italy used on average only 8 kg[4] of nitrogenous fertilizer per hectare, 16 kg of phosphates, and 1 kg of potassium, while the Netherlands used eight times as much nitrogen, four times as much phosphate, and over fifty times as much potassium. In France the use of nitrogen was about the same as in Italy, and that of phosphorus was actually lower, while Germany held an indeterminate position between the two in them both. Adding further to costs was the very high labour force engaged in farming. In 1950 this was 16·4 million which was about one-third of the Community's labour engaged in producing 20 per cent of its Gross

Domestic Product. The greatest labour force, both actually and proportionately was that of Italy, whose 6·5 million employed in farming was about 40 per cent of the country's total labour force and was considerably higher than this in the south of the country. France's 5·2 million constituted about 30 per cent of her labour force, and both of these contrasted with Germany's 9 per cent and the Netherlands 12 per cent.

Table 16. Yields of Some Principal Crops, 1950 and 1965

Product	Germany (FR)	France	Italy	Netherlands	Belgium	Luxembourg	Community
			1950				
Wheat	25·8	17·8	16·5	32·3	31·1	18·2	18·4
Maize	25·5	12·4	15·5	—	35·4	—	15·0(a)
Total Cereals	23·1	15·9	15·7	27·9	29·5	17·0	18·0
Rice (b)	—	31·8	39·5	—	—	—	39·0
Potatoes	244·0	131·0(c)	63·0	240·0	235·0	185·0	179·0
Sugar Beet	362·0	344·0	257·0	435·0	427·0	—	343·0(d)
Permanent Meadows	45·4	33·4	36·6	—	—	33·0	—
			1965				
Wheat	30·8	32·7	22·8	43·6	37·5	25·5	28·7
Maize	35·9	39·1	32·3	—	44·6	—	35·4(a)
Total Cereals	28·2	31·0	23·6	36·5	34·9	25·5	28·5
Rice (b)	—	24·8	30·5	—	—	—	29·3
Potatoes	231·0	195·0	102·0	263·0	250·0	200·0	199·0
Sugar Beet	366·0	429·0	322·0	394·0	388·0	—	381·0(d)
Permanent Meadows	63·4	42·9	57·8	—	78·3	45·8	52·4(a)

(a) Excl. the Netherlands (c) Excl. potatoes grown in market gardens
(b) Husked (d) Excl. Luxembourg.
Source: Statistical Office of the European Community

In the period since the establishment of the Community there have been great improvements in all these things, and they have been most remarkable in those countries, notably Italy and France, which had formerly been in the weakest position. In the Community as a whole cereal yields between 1950 and 1965 increased by two-thirds, sown grass by one-third, and sugar beet and fodder beet by one-tenth. The cereal yields in France actually doubled over this period, in Italy they increased by a half, and similar great increases have been made in the yields of other crops. In the Low Countries with their already high productivity the increases have been on a much smaller scale, and in Belgium the grain yield went up by as little as one-seventh. In Germany there was an average increase in cereal yields of one-fifth, but in fodder crops and vegetables they have remained almost static. This success story has been made possible by many things, notably the increased use of fertilizers. In the Community as a whole their use has gone up by three times per hectare of cultivated land since 1950, and the greatest increases have been again in Italy and France where in each case they have gone up on average four times. Both these countries, however, remain well below Benelux and Germany, and the Netherlands uses six times as much nitrogen and two and a half times as much phosphates per hectare as Italy, although the gap between them has been considerably narrowed. In a similar way, mechanization has been increasing, and although Germany and Benelux remain the most highly mechanized, France is now approaching the Belgian level, although Italy remains very low with only one-sixth of the tractors which Germany has in proportion to its cultivated land.

4. At the same time as yields have been going up, the numbers employed in agriculture have been going down even more spectacularly. In the Community as a whole the agricultural labour force fell from 16·4 million in 1950 to 13·9 million in 1962 and 11·6 million in 1966. While Italy's agricultural population of four millions remains the largest in the Community, it has been reduced by two-thirds since 1950 and now constitutes 25 per cent of the labour force, although it is still double this in many parts of the south. In France only 18 per cent of the labour force is now in agriculture, but the greatest decrease of all has been in Belgium. While in 1950 there were 40,000 more Belgian than Dutch farmers, by 1963 there were 100,000 fewer, and the total Belgian agricultural labour force had been halved. In the Netherlands itself the decrease was only one-quarter, this being due to the relatively high level of mechanization which existed there before.

There have been numerous other changes, including the increased use of insecticides and fungicides and the regrouping of small and uneconomic holdings into larger ones, but the change of most fundamental importance to the nature of the farming has been the gradual decline in the proportion of the land under arable and an increase in that under pasture. Although there has been a decline in grain farming generally, this has not been true of every crop, and while the acreage under rye and oats has gone down considerably, that under wheat and barley has been increasing. There

108

has also been a decline in potatoes, but sugar beet and many types of fodder crops have gone up. Although the actual numbers of livestock have not increased considerably, and those of sheep have actually gone down, there has been a steady increase in the output of meat and milk products resulting from the greater efficiency of the farming. All this is a reflection both of the improved diet of the Community, and the demand for high protein foods, together with the change to a farming which is better able to cater for internal needs.[5]

The Guidance section of the EAGGF (See page 100) is now an active participant in these changes, and is providing direct help to improve farms and marketing facilities. The first improvement grants totalling $9 million were actually made in October 1965, and Italy and Germany have been particular beneficiaries. Projects aided include the construction of dairies, fruit and vegetable-processing plants, slaughterhouses and irrigation works. The 1966-9 programme is costing $672 million, and of this $130 million is allocated to the development of backward farming regions, $100 million to improve the quality and rationalize the distribution of the dairying industry, $90 million to the meat sector, and $80 million to fruit and vegetable marketing. Of the remainder, large amounts will go into irrigation and drainage works, to encourage the better use of farm labour, and to improve the production of olive oil and wine.[6]

Inherent in the rise in the general level of the farming has been an increase in regional specialization to meet the needs of the new large market. Such specialization had, as we have seen, already taken place over wide areas before the Community came into existence, notably in the Netherlands with its concentration on pastoral produce, vegetables and flowers. It was inhibited by the great difficulty of making inroads into foreign markets when marketing arrangements differed so much, there were such fluctuations in price levels, and protective tariffs provided an added discouragement.[7] The free market is now, however, encouraging specialization and each region is increasingly producing those things for which it is particularly well fitted. Thus Italy had been handicapped by poor communications, primitive farming methods and lack of large markets from exploiting its great climatic advantages. The building of the 'Euroroutes', free trade within the Six, and the stabilization of prices are helping to change all this, and together with the injection of capital from Community, government and private sources, this has meant that increasing quantities of fruit, vegetables, oil, wine and rice are now being grown for export. Similarly south-eastern France is specializing in wine, fruit and primeurs, western France in pastoral produce and vegetables, and the Low Countries have reinforced their already high degree of concentration on dairying and market gardening in the north and dairying and grain in the south.

Table 17. Imports and Exports of Foodstuffs, Beverages, and Tobacco, 1965
(Grouped according to SOEC's Tariff Classification)

Country	Imports		Exports	
	Mill. dollars	% of Total Imports	Mill. dollars	% of Total Exports
Germany (FR)	3,651	20·9	435	2·4
France	1,772	17·1	1,599	15·9
Italy	1,611	21·9	850	11·8
Netherlands	988	13·2	1,567	24·5
BLEU	826	13·0	430	6·7

(Source: Statistical Office of the European Community)

This steady increase in regional specialization as a normal feature of agricultural practice is certainly one of the most significant long-term changes now taking place in the Community's agriculture, and it is the aim of CAP to establish the best conditions in which this can take place. A major symptom of this specialization is the great increase in intra-Community trade which, between 1958 and 1965, went up threefold compared with an increase of only three-fifths in the imports of foodstuffs from third countries.[8] The largest exporter is the Netherlands, whose intra-Community exports in 1965 were valued at $750 million, and these were considerably greater than her exports to countries outside the Community. While France now exports nearly as much to the rest of the Community as does the Netherlands, this is, however, only two-thirds as much as her third country exports. Italy's food exports of $7 million are almost equally divided between the Community and third countries, and Belgium now sends the larger part of its much smaller exports to other parts of the Community. The greatest food importer is Germany, which brings in about one-third of its requirements from the Community, and Belgium also brings in just over a third, while France and Italy depend on other Community countries for only about a seventh and a sixth respectively.

The Community as a whole has potentially a high degree of self-sufficiency, and output of the so-called 'temperate foodstuffs'—principally foodgrains, milk products, and meat—in the Six approaches very close to their consumption of these items. In 1965 the 60 million tons of cereals were 84 per cent[9] of the home requirements, the 10 million tons of meat 95 per cent, the $1\frac{1}{2}$ million tons of cheese 98 per cent, and the 1·2 million tons of sugar beet grown were also about equal to producing as much sugar as was consumed. However, the balance of surplus and deficit varies considerably in the individual countries, with the Netherlands having large surpluses of butter, cheese, and beef and a small surplus of sugar, and France producing small surpluses of all these commodities and a larger one of cereals. In contrast to this, both Germany and Italy have deficits in all the main temperate foodstuffs, in the former because population has long outstripped production, and in the latter because the country is ill-adapted to practise much pastoral farming, and even intensive cereal growing is limited. Belgium is comparable with Germany in having a large industrial population to be fed, and it has a deficit in most things, except for sugar beet in which there is a small surplus.

Since the extent of the Community's production is limited by climate, there must always be large imports of such tropical products as tea, coffee, cocoa, and vegetable oils, together with a multitude of other goods ranging from spices to pineapples. Large quantities of these are in fact being supplied by the Community's African associates, and the extent of this trade will be considered later. The imports of temperate foodstuffs is also made larger by the fact that the nations with surpluses sell a great deal of their produce outside the Community. This is both because of the excellent opportunities which frequently exist for sales to other parts of the world, and because for certain commodities the Community market still has a limited capacity which would be totally unable in present circumstances to absorb all the produce put on it. As it is, foodstuffs make up 18 per cent of the Community's total imports, over 20 per cent in the case of Germany and Italy, but only 17 per cent of the French and 13 per cent of those of Benelux. In actual terms, Germany is the largest single importer, taking 40 per cent of the Community total, while the imports of France and Italy make up about 20 per cent each. In 1965 the food exports of the six countries were in value only half the imports, the greatest exporters being France and the Netherlands which together accounted for two-thirds of the total, and of the remainder a half came from Italy.

While the overall features of the agriculture of the Community have been moulded by physical and economic circumstances common to the whole area, its precise emphasis and degree of prosperity have been determined within the framework of each individual nation. This is not only attributable to its technical proficiency but

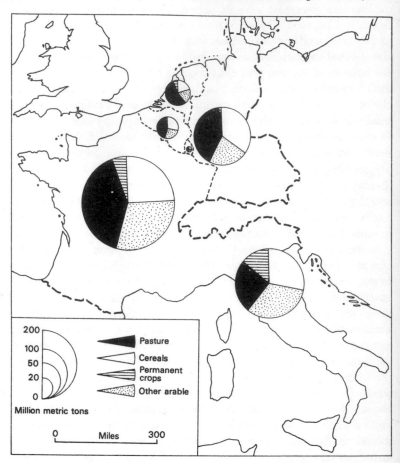

Fig. 26. Land utilization by country 1966.

also to its policy with regard to the supply of foodstuffs. In France and Germany, agricultural development in the early years of the twentieth century fell behind that of industry, and until recent years Italy was backward in both. Only in the Low Countries was there an increase in the level of agricultural productivity and efficiency commensurate with those in other areas of the economy, and in the Netherlands, which at first lacked the wherewithal for industrial growth, agriculture has come to play as important a part as did industry in her neighbours.

This general neglect sprang from the belief that the countries of Western Europe could not hope to feed their huge industrial populations, and that this had to be done through large scale cheap imports, preferably from imperial possessions. Even the countries which retained a considerable capacity for agricultural exports were prevented from supplying their neighbours to any very large extent because of high costs, prejudice against 'foreign' produce and adverse trading policies.

It is the intention of the Common Agricultural Policy to effect a planned transition from independence to interdependence, and to make the Community countries collectively more self-sufficient in the wide range of commodities which they themselves are well adapted to produce. In order to achieve this, the CAP is assisting the process of agricultural modernization, creating a large market with stable prices so as to foster the development of specialist commercial farming, and at the same time, by means of a levy on imports, providing some degree of protection from outside competition.

Yet, in spite of all this, there are still parts of Italy, central France and southern Germany where the level of the farming remains very low. Progress has been stultified by the sheer physical problems of introducing mechanization, the lack of capital, poor communications, and an inability to compete in price with more favoured regions. In addition to this, the drift from the land is greatest in areas such as these, and although it is axiomatic that more efficiency can only be achieved with a much smaller labour force, the draining away of the younger people does not hold out much hope for improvement in the near future. The existence of the Community, by establishing free competition and increasing the mobility of labour, is actually accentuating this process. What is happening therefore is an increase in the differences between the high production and the low production areas, and a concentration of specialist farming in those areas already having a good quality agriculture. The greatest concentration is particularly in Van Valkenburg's high production regions, and the areas outside these will need very special treatment if they are in the long run going to be competitive.

In assessing the contribution of the Community to all this, it is important not to come to the conclusions that *post hoc ergo propter hoc* and attribute all the developments in agriculture to its existence.

There had in any case been a substantial increase in the level of efficiency before the Community came into being, and even greater strides have been made in many other European countries which are not members of the Community. The present ferment in agriculture must be seen as all part of the wider process of achieving greater self-sufficiency now that the old imperial bonds have been severed, and the supply of food and raw materials to the ex-imperial power is no longer as cheap, secure and automatic as it used to be.

With the steady increase of its powers over agriculture, the Community has, however, become more and more an active participant in this process of change, and its greatest contribution has been to stimulate 'self-help' by forcing the national agricultures to become more competitive and to create the right conditions for the evolution of an agriculture tailored to fit the needs of the Six as a whole.[10] Furthermore, it has injected the whole operation with a common purpose within the all-embracing ideal of a united Community.

'The problem of Europe,' said Maurice le Lannou, 'is that of the place of Europe in the world,'[1] and although the Community's work consists essentially of the remodelling of Europe, in the long term it will stand or fall by its relationship to the rest of the world. However, one of the criticisms frequently levelled against it is that it is 'inward-looking'—a league of rich nations intent on making themselves richer and increasingly divorcing themselves from their poorer neighbours. In answer to such critics one must admit that intra-Community economic relations have become closer than those with third countries, and the growth in commercial, industrial, and financial contacts among the Community countries is at a faster rate than that between the Community as a whole and the rest of the world. However, this is all a relative matter and should not be allowed to obscure the magnitude of the Community's world relations in trade, investment, and aid to underdeveloped countries.

In 1966 the Community became the world's largest exporter, a position which it had won from the United States. Total exports to third countries in 1966 were worth $29,500 million which was a rise of 85 per cent over those of 1958. Over 80 per cent of exports are manufactured goods, and four-fifths of these consist of machinery and transport equipment alone, while over a half of the remaining 20 per cent are foodstuffs, in particular wine, cheese, and fruit. Well over a half of all the goods exported went to Western Europe and North America, and the biggest single importers in order of importance were the United States, United Kingdom, Switzerland, Spain, Denmark, and Austria. While the adjacent countries of Western Europe took 42 per cent of all exports, it is significant that the combined total of those sent to Eastern Europe and the Soviet Union made up only an additional 5 per cent (Fig. 30). The rest were widely distributed throughout the world, with the largest slice going to Africa which took 12 per cent and the smallest to the countries of the Far East and Australasia.

The Community's total imports in 1966 were worth $31,200 million, a rise of 93 per cent on their 1958 level. While their world distribution pattern resembles in many ways that of exports,. there are some very significant differences in detail. By far the largest single slice comes from the temperate North Atlantic countries, but it is a smaller one than in the case of exports and makes up less than half the total. The proportions from the two sides of the Atlantic are also very different, and while the value of imports from North America is nearly twice that of exports, those from other West European countries are less than three-quarters of the exports to them. The imports from North America include particularly such things as coal, oil, iron ore, non-ferrous metals, and temperate food-stuffs, and from the other European countries come a wide range of manufactured goods, iron ore (Sweden), wood and pulp (Scandinavia), and fruit (Southern Europe). The largest imports come from the United States, United Kingdom, Sweden, and Switzerland, three of these being also among the largest importers of Community goods. Imports from Eastern Europe and the Soviet Union are mainly of foodstuffs and raw materials, and they make up only a very slightly greater proportion of the total than they did in the case of exports.

Exports to the underdeveloped countries as a whole are considerably exceeded by imports from them, and they account collectively for over one-third of the Community total. There are, however, some exceptions and the opposite is the case with southeast Asia and China, However, this is not really a counterweight since the total trade with this latter group is less than that with Africa alone. Away from the North Atlantic area, Africa and the Middle East are the Community's most important trading partners and together they supply a fifth of the total imports. These consist particularly of petroleum from the Middle East and North Africa, iron ore and other minerals from north-west Africa and the Congo, and tropical products coming mostly from West Africa.

If we consider the relative importance to third countries of trade with the Community, we will find a very different emphasis in the world distribution. For instance, in spite of the large trade which the temperate North Atlantic countries have with the Community, it frequently makes up only a small proportion of their total, and only 17 per cent of British exports, 15 per cent of American and 6 per cent of Canadian are destined for the Six. Similarly 20

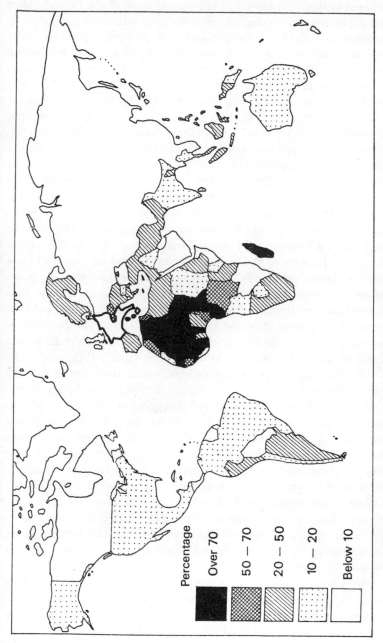

Percentage

Over 70

50 — 70

20 — 50

10 — 20

Below 10

Fig. 27. The Community's share in the imports of the main non-Community countries.

per cent of British imports, 18 per cent of those of the United States and 6 per cent of Canadian come from Community countries. In contrast to this, both Switzerland and Austria have very close trading relations with the Community which supplies around 60 per cent of their imports and takes around 40 per cent of their exports. The proportions in the case of the countries of West and North Africa are usually even higher, with the Community taking well over 60 per cent of their exports, and over 80 per cent of those of Algeria and Senegal. In terms of total trade, however, the Community is more important to the African countries than are the African countries to the Community. This can be clearly seen from the fact that while 43 per cent of total African exports go to the Community, only 7 per cent of those from the Community go to Africa.

The largest increases in external exports have been in those to the Soviet Union and the Eastern European countries, and between 1953 and 1964 those to the Soviet Union alone increased by nearly five times. Exports to the temperate North Atlantic countries have also been going up rapidly, and over the same period they increased threefold. Trade with the underdeveloped countries, however, has in general been increasing at a much slower rate. Exports to Africa went up by 56 per cent and those to South-East Asia by only 33 per cent; the Middle East is the only part of the underdeveloped world to which exports have been growing rapidly (Fig. 28).

Likewise there have been very spectacular increases in imports from Eastern Europe and the Soviet Union, these being mostly foodstuffs and raw materials, but the greatest increase of all has been in manufacturered goods from Japan, although the total trade with this country remains very small and still represents little more than one per cent of the Community's total. There have also been very large increases in imports from the North Atlantic countries, these having been made up particularly of raw materials from North America and both manufactured goods and raw materials from Western Europe. As in the case of exports, imports from the underdeveloped countries have all increased at a much slower rate, with the exception again of the Middle East where they have gone up by over 150 per cent.

The second main aspect of the Community's external economic relations is its aid and overseas investment, but it is impossible to understand the nature and direction of this without first considering the countries with which the Community has association agreements. When the Treaty of Rome was signed, France, Belgium and to a lesser extent the Netherlands still had colonies and dependencies,

118

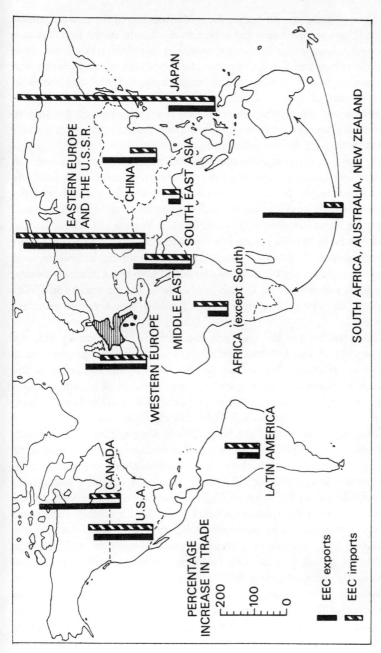

Fig. 28. Exports of EEC countries. Percentage increase by region, 1953–64.

CANADA

U.S.A.

WESTERN EUROPE

EASTERN EUROPE
AND THE U.S.S.R.

CHINA

JAPAN

SOUTH EAST ASIA

MIDDLE EAST

AFRICA (except South)

LATIN AMERICA

SOUTH AFRICA, AUSTRALIA, NEW ZEALAND

PERCENTAGE
INCREASE IN TRADE

200

100

0

EEC exports

EEC imports

119

and it was necessary to define their relationship to the new organization. It was decided that these territories should in the first instance become associates for five years, and that this should, in the words of Article 131 of the Treaty, 'permit the furthering of the interests and prosperity of the inhabitants of these countries and territories in such a manner as to lead them to the economic, social and cultural development which they expect'. To begin the process leading to this desirable end, they were given preference in the Community markets and aid to the value of $581 million.

By 1962 when this agreement ended most of them had become independent and they were given the option of continuing with the association. Out of this came the Yaoundé Convention of 1963 signed by eighteen African states.[2] Except for two, Madagascar and Somalia, these are contiguous countries in West and Central Africa, and sixteen of them were ex-French colonies which had gained their independence in 1960 and the Congo, an ex-Belgian colony, had become independent in the same year. The remaining signatory, Somalia, was in part an Italian colony until the Second World War and on the strength of this asked for and was granted associate status.[3]

The total area of the eighteen associates is 11 million sq. km, ten times that of the Community itself, but their total population is only 60 million, a third that of the latter. The disparity in the national products is even greater, and the total of all the African associates together is under three per cent of that of the Community, or less than a half that of the Netherlands alone.

The declared aim of the association Convention is to 'further the economic diversification and industrialization of the associated states in order to permit them to strengthen their economic equilibrium and independence'. To this end the Community has agreed to provide aid to the value of $730 million over the five-year period from 1964 to 1969, plus another $70 million for other associated states which are still dependent on one or other Community country. This represents a total increase of 38 per cent over the assistance granted in the first five-year period, and $620 million of it is in the form of grants for improvements and technical aid, the remaining $110 million being for developing the infrastructure of communications, water supplies, and schools and to help diversify production. Money can also be made available for stabilizing prices in cases where fluctuation would do damage to a nation's economy as a whole. The programme is being handled by the European Development Fund, which decides the projects to be aided and how the aid is to be used, and a new feature which was absent from the first association agreement is the participation of the European Investment Bank which provides loans at a specially reduced rate of interest.[4] To the end of 1966 the EIB had actually financed three loans worth $3·4 million in Cameroon and Ivory Coast.

Aid provided under agreements between the Community as a whole and the associated countries does not include that provided under bilateral agreements made between individual members of the Community and individual developing countries. In addition to the $581 million provided by the Community as such in the five years 1958–62, the Six also gave $6,823 million to the developing countries in general on a bilateral basis. Of this $4,292 million came from France, $1,755 million from Germany, $322 million from Belgium, $235 million from Italy and $220 million from the Netherlands.

The other great advantage which the associate states enjoy is unrestricted entry into the Community for their exports. The tropical products and raw materials that they send are in any case vital to the Community, but this absence of tariffs puts the associates at a great advantage as compared with their competitors in other parts of the tropical world. Their economies have in most cases been built up especially to serve the French and Belgian markets, so that their present trading pattern is largely the continuation of the one they inherited from colonial days. With the one exception of Somalia, all the associates conduct a very high proportion of their trade with Community countries, the highest being Senegal, Ivory Coast, Gabon, and the Congo Republic. On balance the Community countries provide over 60 per cent of their imports and take 70 per cent of their exports, and the greatest part of this trade is with the major ex-imperial power, France, which in 1965 was the recipient of over three-fifths of the Community's imports from the associated states and the source of three-quarters of all the goods they imported from the Community. However, even these proportions are smaller than those of a few years back. Now other countries, notably Germany and Italy, are increasing their trade with the associates and have doubled its value between 1962 and 1965. In spite of all this, trade with the associates still makes up only a small part of the Community's total and currently accounts for 6 per cent of her exports and 7 per cent of imports. In the case of five of the Community countries the proportion is actually much smaller still, but to the remaining one, France, they are the source of a fifth of her imports and take over a fifth of her exports.

While the associates get tariff-free entry for their exports into the Community, the agreement does not automatically give the Community states a similar right to unrestricted entry into the markets of the associates, who may impose tariffs against Community manufactured goods so as to protect their own industries. All that is required is that the Community exporters should be given certain preferences over their competitors from the other industrial nations.

It is notable that the other African countries with the highest trade dependence on the Community are the ex-French colony of Algeria, the two former French protectorates of Morocco and Tunisia, and the ex-Italian colony of Libya. In the case of all except Algeria, the association with the former colonial power had ended before the signing of the Treaty of Rome, and Algeria, on gaining independence in 1962 chose not to retain the association. However, the proportion of its trade with France has remained very large, and has considerably increased since the early 1960s as a result of the discovery of new reserves of oil, natural gas, and iron ore and their export across the Mediterranean. The proportion of its external trade with the Community is now higher than that of any other country.

In July 1966 Nigeria became the first new African state to be made an associate, although this did not give her all the privileges of the Yaoundé Convention agreement. Instead of unrestricted entry for her exports into the Community, she is given tariff-free quotas, but only on palm oil, rubber, groundnuts, and cocoa. She was impelled into seeking associate status by the fact that trade with the Community is more important to her than to any other African Commonwealth country, accounting for about a third of her exports and a quarter of her imports.

The two European associates are Greece and Turkey admitted in 1962 and 1963 respectively. After the creation of the Community, followed by that of the Free Trade Association (EFTA), these were two of the only four countries of non-Communist Europe which were left out in the cold, and they were quick to remedy this situation by gravitating into the Community orbit. They had a great deal to gain from this, both because of the nature of their trade and their overall economic situation. Trade with the Community is very important to them both, and accounts for 41 per cent of Greek imports and 37 per cent of her exports; in the case of Turkey the proportions are 28 per cent and 34 per cent respectively. Their principal exports to the Community are fruit, grain, and tobacco, in return for which they take mainly manufactured goods. They are also both exporters of labour, which can be absorbed, thanks to the agreements, by the Community's industries.

Since Turkey and Greece are both poor nations, another urgent need is investment for industrial development, and the activities of

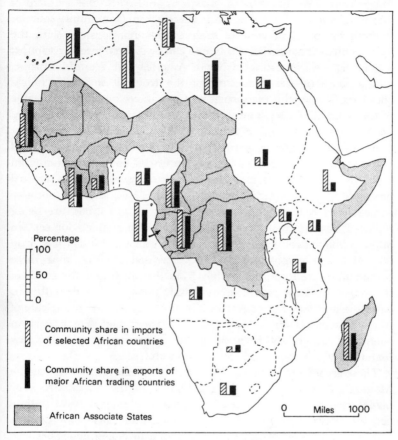

Fig. 29. The African Associates.

the EIB have been extended to them.[5] Up to the end of 1965 seventeen different projects had been aided, eight of these in Greece and nine in Turkey, to a total value of $90 million. Among the most important of the Turkish projects have been a wire-drawing factory at Ismit, a dam and hydroelectric station at Keban, a power station at Kovada lake, and a nylon thread factory at Bursa, and in Greece there have been a number of irrigation works, a cement factory at Eleusis and a nitro-phosphate fertilizer factory at Salonica.

The major economic sphere of the Community is, therefore, an area which focuses on the North Atlantic Ocean, comprising Western Europe, North and Central America, Northern Africa and the Middle East (Fig. 30). This area handles over two-thirds of its imports and three-quarters of its exports, and is also the recipient of all the aid and investment coming directly from Community sources.

From the point of view of their trading relationships with the Community the countries of this area can be divided into two groups: a northern tier consisting of North America and Western Europe, and a southern tier made up of the tropical and sub-tropical countries. Trade with the former group is about four times the value of that with the latter, and, with certain notable exceptions, it has been increasing far more rapidly, This change in the respective shares of the two groups is due largely to the increasing exchange of manufacturered goods among the industrial countries, compared with the much slower increase in their consumption of tropical products. This is in part a matter of rate of consumption, but also in part because some tropical products, such as rubber, are being replaced by synthetic materials. However, the demand for certain other primary products, particularly petroleum, natural gas, iron ore, and non-ferrous metals, has increased rapidly, and these commodities are imported widely from the north and the south of the major economic sphere, so increasing the overall trade within it. After the northern tier countries, the most rapidly expanding rate of trade is with certain of the Middle Eastern and North African countries, principally because of the increasing supplies of raw materials which they send to the Community.

Those areas immediately adjacent to the Community, such as the Maghreb to the south and Scandinavia to the north, are very obvious sources of raw materials on account of their natural resources, their proximity, and their traditional trade links, but Eastern Europe, which is even nearer, has been of little consequence because of the coolness of political relations. In recent years the political climate has warmed up considerably, and this has been reflected in the rapid increases in trade both with this area and with the Soviet Union.

In contrast with this the tendency has been, as we have seen, for trade between the developed and the underdeveloped countries to decrease in importance, and together with this there has been a widening in the gulf of national products and living standards between the two. The Community's relationship with the 'Yaoundé Eighteen' is an attempt to bridge this gap by assuring their markets

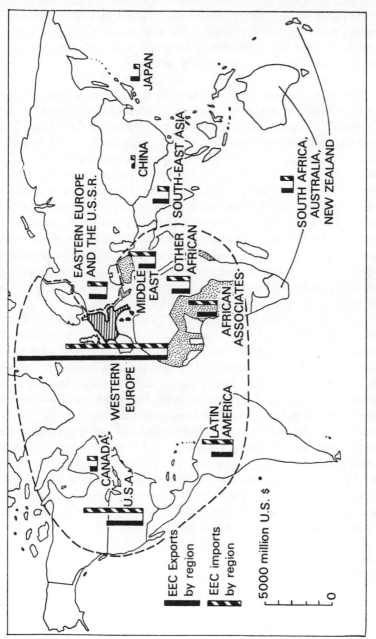

Fig. 30. International trade of the Community by world regions.

EASTERN EUROPE
AND THE U.S.S.R.

CHINA

JAPAN

SOUTH-EAST ASIA

OTHER
AFRICAN

MIDDLE
EAST

AFRICAN
ASSOCIATES

SOUTH AFRICA,
AUSTRALIA,
NEW ZEALAND

WESTERN
EUROPE

CANADA,
U.S.A.

LATIN
AMERICA

EEC Exports
by region

EEC imports
by region

5000 million U.S. $

0

and providing aid to their economies. The new dependence of the Community on imports of petroleum, iron ore and other metals is serving to strengthen the trade links with those African countries which are able to supply them, although many of these, notably Algeria and Libya, are not actually associates.

It is quite apparent that neither the label 'inward-looking' nor 'outward-looking' are particularly true or final descriptions of the Community today. In almost all countries there is a bit of both, but here the contrasts between the two are more marked and in some ways paradoxical. This is the world's largest single trading bloc, but about 40 per cent of the trade of the individual countries is actually conducted with one another. While its world trade has been increasing very rapidly, its internal trade is increasing three times as fast, and while it is annually becoming more dependent on imports of certain commodities, it is rapidly attaining a high degree of self-sufficiency in many others. Furthermore, while its common external tariff is designed principally to protect home industries, it is from the industrial countries that its greatest imports come and manufactures make up the largest single sector of imported goods.

Every major trend in the Community's external economic relations is thus balanced by a countervailing trend, and the overall movement towards greater self-sufficiency is balanced by long-term planning on the assumption of the existence of permanent or semi-permanent deficiencies. The keynote of the whole process is a greater selectivity in the goods imported, in the regions from which they are imported and in the choice of countries to benefit from Community aid and investment. This geographical concentration is the counterpart on the external plane of the changes which we have already observed taking place internally. Just as the Community is itself a symptom of increased regional consciousness, so its external economic relations are evolving in a regional pattern, and this is becoming more emphasized as the Community makes its impact as an independent entity on the world scene.

8 The Logic of Unity

The countries of the Community originally decided to enter into an economic merger for a variety of reasons, but, particularly in the case of those five of them which are part of trunk Europe, their motivation was based on a very real geographical unity. The shatter belt of political frontiers which extends through its centre from the Rhine delta to the Alps coincides only in one place with a linguistic boundary, and almost everywhere divides areas which are physically, economically, and frequently culturally single units. Most basic of all is the essential unity of the Triangle and its associated areas which has been, in the words of the Schuman Declaration, 'always prescribed by geography, always prevented by history', and the Community has given this unity formal expression.

The conditions produced by its establishment have contributed to both centrifugal and centripetal changes in its industrial geography. As a consequence of changed economic conditions assisted by the positive policy of the Community there have been important industrial developments in formerly unimportant regions. The changed conditions include the harnessing of new forms of home-produced power, the renewed exploitation of home resources, and the great improvements in communications which have increased the accessibility of the remoter areas. Central and southern Italy, southern France and parts of Bavaria have been notable beneficiaries from this.

The centripetal changes have led to concentration into the most favoured regions, and, as we have already observed, it is around the Rhinelands that this has been most in evidence. The economic unification of this great area is certainly one of the most significant results of the Community, since up to then it had been the archetype of artificial fragmentation of a natural unit.

The Rhine rises in Switzerland and then forms the Franco-German frontier for 160 km. It then flows through Germany, finally bending westward to reach the sea in the Netherlands, although a part of its composite delta is in Belgium, and many of its left-bank tributaries, notably the Moselle and the Meuse, flow through eastern France. The Rhineland area is geographically the Community's keystone, and its economic unification is essential for the welding together of the six nations. This area has always been a delectable prize, but with large scale industrialization during the nineteenth century it became more alluring than ever to the neighbouring powers.[1] It is rich in coal, iron ore, hydro-carbons, lignite, and chemicals. In 1938 the area within the Rhine drainage basin produced 230 millions tons of hard coal, this being 85 per cent of the combined output of the six countries within whose territory is it located. In the same year it produced about 14 million tons of iron ore concentrate and 28 million tons of steel, these being 95 per cent and 85 per cent of the national totals respectively.

Yet in spite of this great wealth and importance, it has never succeeded in developing into a major centre of political power. With the break-up of Charlemagne's empire much of it had a transitory existence as part of Lotharingia, but it was not defensible enough to last very long, and it has come through history as a political shatter belt which has been both the cause of wars and the cockpit in which they have been fought. Out of this came the desire of the riparian countries to minimize their dependence on the Rhinelands. Germany built the port of Emden and connected it to the Ruhr with the Dortmund-Ems canal, at the same time increasing the trade of her North Sea ports and decreasing the flow through the Rhine mouths which were out of her direct political control. Canalization projects of the Rhine and its tributaries were shelved, and a deliberate policy was adopted of encouraging industrial development further east. France, for her part, was exploiting her small and poor coalfields in the Massif Central, while paying less attention to the far greater assets in her section of the Rhine basin. In spite of all this, the economic evolution of Western Europe was inevitably making the Rhinelands more important than ever before.

In an attempt to delimit with any degree of precision the extent of the Community super-core, the significance of a number of elements must be evaluated, particularly the population, industry, resources, energy supplies, and general economic trends.

As a result of a survey of its population, I. B. Kormoss has come to the conclusion that the Community's demographic heart consists of the area delimited by a line from just north of Boulogne, south-eastward to Metz and Nancy, then on southward to Belfort and skirting the Swiss border to Würzburg and Wolfsburg in West Germany, finally bending westward into the Low Countries[2] (Fig. 31). The area thus enclosed has about 20 per cent of the Community's area, but 40 per cent of its population, and in 1959 this totalled 63 million. The population is very unevenly distributed, and approximately one twelfth of its area has a density of below 50 per square kilometre, less than one-fifth the average for the area. The main concentrations of population are aligned in two directions, following the coalfield belt and the Rhine respectively. The two meet at the Ruhr, and the Land of Nordrhein-Westfalen, which is basically the Ruhr region, has a population of 15·7 million—nearly a quarter that of the whole central population area.

The greatest concentrations of industry are also to be found within approximately this same area. Three—or four if we include Luxembourg—of the national economic core regions are within it, as are also the highly industrialized lands of central Belgium, the south-east Netherlands and eastern France.[3] The major industrial zone is built around the Rhine and its larger tributaries from the delta to the rift valley, and here the greatest variety of means of communication follow the same routeway. It makes up the northern part of the Lotharingian axis, and the great ports at its junction with the sea handle a half of the Community's seaborne commerce.

There is also a broad correspondence with the northern section of the Home Energy Production zone. Within this are produced a very large proportion of the Community's output of fossil fuels— coal, lignite, natural gas, and petroleum—and the area has an overwhelming dominance as a source of home energy supplies. Besides this the lower Rhineland is the Community's most important oil importing and refining region.

Quite clearly, therefore, this Rhineland region dominates the Community in most particulars, and its centre, the Community super-core, is the great arc stretching eastward from the lands of the Rhine-Scheldt delta down into the Rhine rift valley (Fig. 32). This includes most of the core regions of the Netherlands, Belgium, and Germany, and is responsible for the production of a good part of the Community's coal, steel, refined oil, transport equipment, general engineering products, chemicals and textiles. Conditions are not uniformly good throughout it, since it contains many of the Community's declining industries as well as those which are now expanding. Its old economic heart is the central industrial belt based on the coalfields and it is from there that expansion has taken place to the coasts and to adjacent parts of the interior. Those industries favouring the coasts are particularly the ones using imported raw materials and those going to the interior are mostly concerned with general manufacturing.

A special index of the importance of this area is the amount of new industrial investment which has been going into it, and this is particularly marked with foreign investment which does not have the inhibitions that sometimes make Community firms slow to relocate when it means moving into the territory of another member state. Of the $29,756 million of direct American investment in the Community's industry between 1958 and 1965, $11,405 million went to West Germany alone and the favourite sites were those in the Rhinelands (Table 18). Of the rest most of that to Belgium and the Netherlands went to those parts within the core, and although

Table 18. US Direct Investments in Common Market Countries 1958, 1962 and 1965 in million $

Country	1958	1962	1965
Germany (FR)	666	1,476	2,417
France	546	1,030	1,584
Italy	280	554	972
Netherlands	207	376	698
Belgium and Luxembourg	208	286	585
Community	1,908	3,722	6,254

(Source: Office of Business Economics, U.S. Department of Commerce)

most of the investment into France went elsewhere, a large part was invested in Alsace. This is reflected in the way in which so many of the principal American companies operating in the Community have such a preference for locations in the super-core above all others. This preference antedates the establishment of the Community since sites in this area have a great deal to commend them in terms of purely national considerations, but with the Community as a whole in mind the preference has become even stronger. It is the combination of optimum conditions in all aspects of supply, production and distribution that have made this region so attractive to industralists, and in the absence of restrictions it will undoubtedly continue to be the recipient of a disproportionate amount of foreign investment. The Community companies themselves, based as they are still on national markets, have been slower to relocate drastically, but with the drift to the west in Germany and the consolidation of industry in the Randstad and mid-Belgium the concentration into the super-core has steadily become more marked. The Rhine rift valley, at its southern end, is the hub of the Community's communications system, and in recent years it has

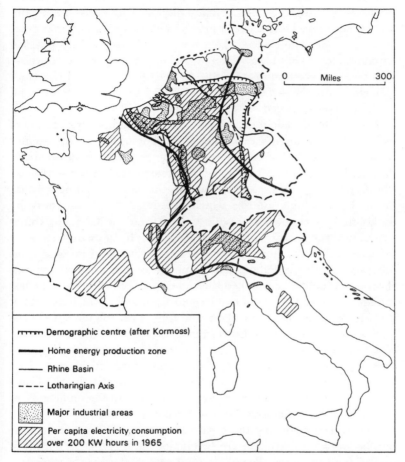

Fig. 31 Criteria used in delimiting the Community super-core region

developed rapidly, particularly for multi-component metal manufactures.[4]

Prior to the establishment of the Community, the super-core, split as it was between four different countries and three different customs unions, was far from constituting an economic unit, since the economies of the politically separated territories were artificially tied to outside areas and were largely unrelated to one another. National frontiers were great gulfs which not only prevented contacts, but were also usually inimical to industrial development in their vicinities. It thus totally lacked the functional completeness which characterizes the developed national core region, reaching its fullest expression in the primate city such as Paris or London. Sir Halford Mackinder wrote nearly sixty years ago of 'that great capital of the Rhinelands which owing to historical and physical circumstances has been dissipated among competing towns— Amsterdam, Rotterdam, Ghent, Brussels, Antwerp, Liège and Cologne'.[5] In place of this dissipation a core region on a continental scale has now emerged.

Looked at in geopolitical terms the pan-Europe movement, of which the most tangible expression is the Community, is an attempt to achieve peacefully from the centre what peripherally based power has been unable to do by force. The greatest impetus to setting up the Community has come from within this latter-day Lotharingia: from the Benelux countries which antedated the Community by establishing their own economic union; from the German Rhinelands, now the heart of the Federal Republic; from the industrialists of eastern France whose existence is so closely bound up with what happens across the Rhine; and from the provinces of Alsace and Lorraine which have changed their nationality four times in the last hundred years as the Franco-German frontier has oscillated. In it the idea of nationality is weakest, and from it have come some of the greatest exponents of the European ideal. Through the unity of the Community these lands are now coming into their own in a way they have not done for over a thousand years, in fact not since Charlemagne's capital was at Aachen. Correspondingly, the Community can become a going concern only through the unification of this area and by building the new Europe around it.

Yet while recognizing the great importance of this core, it must not be forgotten that there are two major industrial areas outside it —Paris and the upper Po valley—and each of these is the economic core of its own country. The upper Po region is allied closely to the core by the ever more efficient communications along the Lotharingian axis, the grand trunk route of the Community, and although the Alps remain a formidable barrier they are getting steadily less so. Paris, on the other hand, has evolved as both the political and economic core of a highly centralized country, and its industrial contacts with the super-core are not very great.[6] The communications between the two are nothing like on the scale of those found within the Lotharingian axis. Paris looks far more towards the coast, with which it is connected by the Seine routeway, and the whole area is now an industrial complex quite independent of the super-core. Although not able to rival the latter in production it has a general industrial output and inherent attractiveness to investment second only to it in the Community.

Chisholm has suggested that the major European industrial-region is being consolidated inside a line joining Le Havre, Paris, Strasbourg, Frankfurt, Dortmund, and Amsterdam.[7] This includes the super-core and the eastern part of the Paris basin, but as a concept of the 'major industrial region' of the future this appears to have less validity than that of an extension of the super-core along the Lotharingian axis.

To Bismarck, immersed in late nineteenth-century realpolitik, Europe was no more than a geographical expression, and the idea of a united continent an 'untenable fiction'. Today, as a result of what André Malraux has called the 'ridimensiamento', continents have replaced countries as the most effective units of power, and the achievement of an united Europe has moved from the sphere of ideals through that of practical possibility and has now become a necessity. It is the purposeful coordination of resources on a vast scale which has given the United States and the Soviet Union such power, and the potential—by no means always fulfilled—to raise the standards of living of all their peoples.

The European Community as already functioning is reaching out towards the status of an economic super-power, but it is still far from being a super-power in the full sense since the constituent countries refuse to merge their political and defence structures. It has been said that the theory of the Community is based upon a recognition of the economic importance of the political frontier and of the political importance of the economic frontier,[8] and these two aspects of a nation's life have to be in unison if they are to be meaningful. Economic integration is the basis of political integration, and it is even now in process of removing national sovereignty not by a direct frontal assault but by steady erosion at the foundations. It is this process of fusion at the economic level which is designed, in the words of the Schuman Declaration of 1950 to 'ensure that war becomes not only unthinkable but materially impossible'. This is the theme which has run through the whole of the Community ideal and has made it both a way of resolving national conflicts and of creating a territorial unit more adapted than are the individual nations to the needs of the second half of the twentieth century. It was this which could enable Professor Hallstein to say with complete truth, 'We are not in business—we are in politics'.

In spite of the continued existence of tendencies to nationalism, more pronounced in some of the member states than in others, the

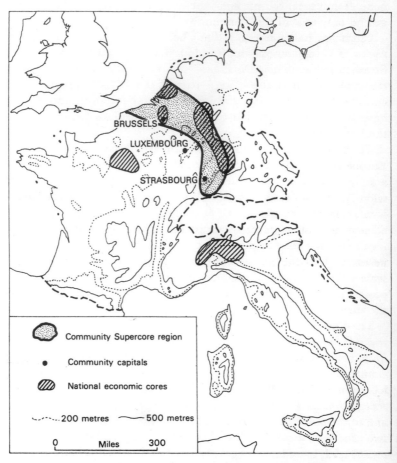

BRUSSELS

LUXEMBOURG

STRASBOURG

🟤 Community Supercore region

● Community capitals

▨ National economic cores

‑‑‑‑‑ 200 metres ——— 500 metres

0   Miles   300

Fig. 32. The Community super-core region

great strides already made have rendered a return to economic nationalism a very difficult business, and the longer the process continues, the more difficult it will become. As we have seen, the new pattern of relations between the Six has now been imprinted on the economic geography, and this is something very difficult to remove. Treaties and agreements have, unfortunately, often proved to be little more than scraps of paper to be torn up as occasion

134

demanded, but it is more difficult to move an oil refinery or a steel plant or to alter the nature of a communications network.

Throughout the foregoing chapters an attempt has been made to assess the degree to which patterns of economic geography have been changing, and to establish the part played by the Community in bringing this about. It is frequently difficult to evaluate with any degree of precision the positive rôle of the Community as an agent of economic change, and to distinguish this from the general trends which might in any case have been anticipated. Since the Community was set up so soon after the Second Word War, it is not possible to say whether the processes of economic integration preceded it, but one can certainly assume that, to some extent at least, they would have occurred in any case, since industrial countries outside it have also been drawn together in a similar way. [9]

However, it is certain that without it the process would have been on a much more limited scale. The abolition of internal restrictions to trade, aid to declining regions and industries, together with regional and transport policies have all given the process of integration an infrastructure on which to operate, a direction and a psychological boost which it would not otherwise have had. 'Europe' has become a tenable reality, and as though to prove it there have come the 'Euro-' businesses, banks, manufacturers, merchants, and hauliers whose natural economic environment is the Community as a unit. This, perhaps more than anything else, is the key to the success of the Community: it is not only that it has fostered conditions for the flourishing of industry which could not have been brought about without it; it is that it has made these conditions permanent and enabled all economic activities to rely on this in making their plans. The great new industrial relocation which is now taking place is a symptom of this, and the infrastructure to make it practicable is being designed on a Community scale.

Yet while the Community is moving towards the condition of a super-power—and it has the sort of industrial structure which could make this possible—it does not have anything like the degree of self-sufficiency possessed by the United States and the Soviet Union. As we have seen, it is very dependent on imports for a great variety of materials, notably petroleum, iron ore, non-ferrous metals, most natural fibres, and a great range of tropical products, and in many of these the degree of dependence is increasing. Thus the Community's relations with the rest of the world, and particularly the underdeveloped world must remain of great importance to her, and the idea of 'turning her back' on the poorer nations is hardly realistic. One of the things which helped the European nations to make the necessary psychological adjustment to go ahead with the Community was the disappearance of their empires and the political dissociation from the former colonies which this entailed. It is now in the economic sphere that relations with these and like countries will be conducted, but they remain essential to the success of the enterprise.

The Community is the result of a 'volte face' in geopolitical relationships which has totally transformed the West European scene in a bare two decades. It is the commencement of the fading from the map of what Henri Brugmans has called the 'états polychromes', into which this part of Europe has been for so long divided and which has had an obsessive influence upon the conduct of affairs.[10] Economic and political stability has been increasingly established in what was until recently one of the world's most wartorn places, and, strangely enough, it has been built around the area which was the continent's main danger zone but now has become its greatest source of strength.

Has the great success of the Community been due to the dedication of a few great 'Europeans', the acquiescence of a chastened Germany, a horror of the past, or is it just an accident? Perhaps all these things have made their contribution, but its success is firmly founded in the close interdependence of these six contiguous countries, and this in turn is based upon the nature of their geographical environment.

9 Britain and the Community

'England—that utmost corner of the west.' King John II i

'These islands, for good or ill, are much more nearly in the centre of the lands of the world than ever before.' J. Fairgrieve. *Geography and World Power.*

The first of these quotations was written in the late sixteenth century and the second in the early part of the twentieth. Far from being mutually contradictory, as might at first appear, they are true for their periods and together reveal the profound change in geographical values which took place during the three centuries which separate them. In the time of Shakespeare England was still a small country on the edge of Europe, while by the late nineteenth century she had become in many ways its most vigorous part, dominating the trade and ocean routeways of the world. In the years since the Second World War, further changes in geographical values have been drawing this country towards the European continent, and this has given rise to the widespread desire for membership of the Community.

The British feeling of being 'a world apart' culminated in the nineteenth century with the era of 'splendid isolation'. In spite of the buffeting which this had received both in war and in peace, Britain was still very unwilling in the early 1950's to throw her weight completely behind the idea of an united Europe, and the attitude of mind of 'storm in Channel—continent isolated' retained a powerful hold. It is notable that in his now famous speech at Zürich in 1946, considered by many to have been a landmark in the European movement, Winston Churchill referred to Britain not as part of the new Europe, but as one of its 'friends and sponsors'. When, a few years later, the Six began to weld themselves together, Britain at first viewed the new grouping with some suspicion, and indeed it would have been surprising had it been otherwise, since this country's traditional policy has been to discourage the emergence of a power of continental dimensions on the other side of the Channel.

The detachment of Britain from the continent is founded upon three underlying geographical factors: physical separation, natural wealth, and maritime location. These must be considered more fully if we are to understand the background to Britain's present relationship with the Community.

Great Britain's insularity has put her in the happy position of benefiting from proximity to the continent while at the same time being free from many of the problems which have beset the continent. Paramount among these is security, and given control of the seas this country has been able to protect herself with the expenditure of a far smaller amount of the national effort than has been necessary for the continental nations, and with a far greater degree of success. The Channel has, therefore, been used as a kind of economic and political sieve, keeping out certain things while allowing others through.

The use of the Channel in this way was made possible by the organization of the island's wealth, which after the later eighteenth century came to be founded principally on its coal, iron, and non-ferrous metals, and, when the supplies of these latter became insufficient, upon coal alone. Britain was not, of course, unique in possessing coal, but the ease with which it could be mined and its high quality combined with other things to produce the conditions in which industry could flourish. So long as coal was the normal source of industrial energy and Britain was unique in possessing the combination of abundant exploitable reserves, internal political and economic stability and a relatively advanced technology, she was the world's leading industrial nation, and remained so until overhauled by the United States and Germany in the late nineteenth century.

In the early nineteenth century the growing imbalances of the country's economy were corrected by imports of raw materials and the disposal overseas of surplus industrial goods to pay for them. This she was able to do with ease, initially by expanding trade with the Americas, her position as a maritime outpost of Europe making her especially well-fitted to conduct this trade since the shortest routes across the Atlantic from North America to North-West Europe terminate at British ports. Later on, when trade with Asia and Africa became more important, she was able to capitalize on the impetus given by her early start. With the exception of coal exports, trade with Europe became steadily less important, and the basic overseas trading pattern of the nineteenth century resolved

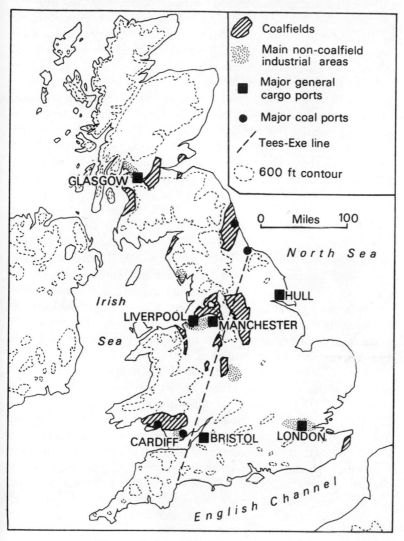

Fig. 33. Industrial Britain in the 1900s

itself into the export of manufactures and the import of raw materials and foodstuffs.

The three attributes of insularity, indigenous wealth, and maritime location have now ceased to carry the weight they have done in the past, and in many ways they have become disadvantages. While the Channel is no defence against modern aircraft and missiles, it is still a considerable hindrance to surface communication with the continent. Nevertheless, it is of no consequence to communications by air, radio and telephone which during the past generation have been doing so much to fill in the psychological Channel between this country and the Community.

As to the second asset, Britain's natural wealth, this is today of much diminished value, and while the major indigenous resource, coal, still supplies the greater part of the home-produced energy, it is becoming steadily less important. Energy supplies have now been added to food and raw materials as items which have to be imported in large quantities. This situation is analogous to that existent in the Community, and apart from energy, in which Great Britain still remains the more self-sufficient, this country has been dependent on large-scale imports for far longer and to a far greater extent than have even the most industrialized of the Community countries.

However, while Great Britain no longer has the wealth and the insularity upon which her great power was built and protected, her central location in regard to the world's land hemisphere remains of great importance to her commerce, and this is demonstrated by the importance of London in international air communications. However, the real geographical centre of the land hemisphere is Brittany, and the advantage of centrality is one which is shared with the adjacent parts of the continent.

With the disintegration of the British Empire, the large slice of trade which was under direct British political control has now become subject to international difficulties which could endanger it. The closures of the Suez canal in 1956 and 1967 together with the Arab oil embargo of the latter year have demonstrated this clearly, and it is desirable that the sources of as many of the nation's imports as possible should be diversified. Besides this the absorbative capacity of Commonwealth and other traditional British markets, and especially those of them classed as underdeveloped countries, is a very limited one, and it is thus necessary to find new outlets for our exports.

Thus it can be seen that the assets which have for so long combined to make Britain both splendid and isolated have either disappeared, or are now of much diminished significance, and this entails the end of the world rôle which they made possible. At the same time a new set of circumstances has arisen, which has in recent years been binding this country more closely to the continent. It was a realization of these which motivated the move to seek association with the Community in the late 1950s, and, when this proved impossible, to come to an agreement with the remaining nations of Western Europe. As a consequence in 1959 the European Free Trade Association (EFTA) was established which bound Great Britain, the four Scandinavian countries, Switzerland, Austria, and Portugal to remove all restrictions to mutual trade over a period of years. Since then trade among these countries has increased rapidly, and in 1965 they took 14 per cent of Britain's exports and supplied 13 per cent of her imports. In January 1967 EFTA became a completely tariff-free area, and this acted as a further stimulation to trade and to other economic contacts among its members.

In spite of the fact that Britain is still not a member of the Community, contacts have nevertheless been growing stronger.[1] This has been occurring in a great variety of ways, principally through trade, finance, industry, and changes in the regional balance of economic activity which have brought about radical changes in the economic geography on either side of the Channel.

Britain's trade with the Community has been rising faster than has her world trade as a whole. Between 1957 and 1965 her exports and imports rose by about 40 per cent, while over the same period the exports to the Community increased by 80 per cent and imports nearly doubled. This has brought up the Community's share in Britain's exports from 15 per cent to 20 per cent and of imports from 12 per cent to 17 per cent. Over the same period the proportions to the Commonwealth countries have been going down from 36 per cent to 30 per cent of imports and from 38 per cent to 29 per cent of exports. Similarly trade with other European countries and with North America has been increasing rapidly, but that with the South American and Asian countries has increased only slowly. This is all part of the reorientation of British trade towards the more rapidly expanding markets, and away from those with small expansion rates which had previously been taking an over-high proportion of exports.

Well over four-fifths of all the exports to the Community countries are of manufactured goods, particularly transport equipment, machinery, domestic appliances, and chemicals. Of the remainder the largest group are coal and refined petroleum products. The composition of this trade is very much in line with the anticipated exports, but it is the imports from the Community which differ from the traditional types of British imports, since over a half are of manufactured goods consisting substantially of the same sorts of things as this country is exporting. This proportion of manufactures is much higher than is found in British imports generally where they make up about one-third of the total, and it again demonstrates that the great increases in trade between Britain and the other

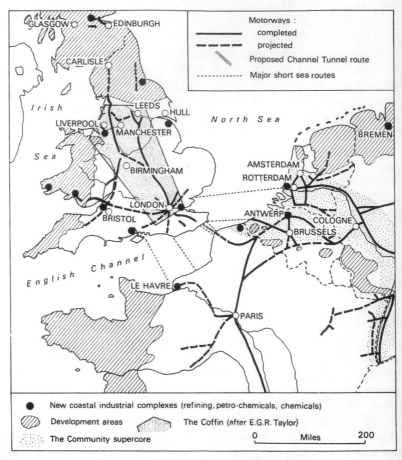

Fig. 34. Britain and Europe: the 1960s

industrial countries is made up largely of the sort of goods which they all make but for which they each have expanding markets. Since for the most part such goods can hardly be described as basic essentials, however important they have become to the nations concerned, the consumer is only too ready to have the wide choice provided by competing firms in various countries. The next largest category of imports from the Community is that of foodstuffs,

142

particularly pastoral products and meat, and the imports from this source have also been increasing at a faster rate than those from the rest of the world.

Another significant development is the establishment of Community firms in Britain and British firms in the Community. The scale of this can be seen from the distribution of British motor vehicle and component factories in the Community (Fig. 19). Similarly British oil refining, chemical and engineering firms are operating alongside Community ones, and the amount of British direct investment in the Community is now £350 million, which is nearly £100 million more than that of ten years ago.[2]

On another level there are the agreements between British and Community firms and organizations to pool technical and financial resources for specific projects. A notable example is the Concorde supersonic airliner being built jointly by Sud Aviation and the British Aircraft Corporation, and there are also other Anglo-French aircraft schemes. At a governmental level there is cooperation with Community countries in CERN for research into high energy physics, ESRO for space research, ELDO for the construction of large rockets, and the United Kingdom Atomic Energy Authority's joint research agreements with Euratom.

These changes in the country's external economic relations have been accompanied by equally impressive and significant ones in the arrangement of its internal economic geography. Britain can be divided on a physical basis into a Highland zone in the north and west and a Lowland zone in the south and east, and they are traditionally separated by the 'Tees-Exe line' (Fig. 33). At the beginning of the present century the main industrial centres were on or near the coalfields along the edges between the two zones. The most important of these areas faced westward and were well connected with the Atlantic by the great ports of Bristol, Liverpool, Glasgow, and, after the completion of the Ship Canal in 1898, Manchester. East and south-east England was quite decidedly an economic backwater with the exception of London, which, although an important industrial city, was principally the business and financial centre for the imperial government.

During the present century, however, a development has occurred analogous to that observed in the Community, resulting principally from the decreased importance of coal and coinciding with the rise of a new group of industries which have not been attracted to the coalfields. These initially established themselves in lowland England. particularly in the neighbourhoods of London and Birmingham, the two major existing industrial centres in it. By the 1930s the older industrial regions were fast declining, both relatively and actually, with the one exception of Merseyside, which continued to retain a high degree of prosperity on account of the diversity of its industrial structure and its good communications with the English Plain. Writing in 1940 Professor E. G. R. Taylor labelled the zone joining Merseyside with the London area 'The Coffin'—ostensibly on account of its shape—and showed how it had become the country's most important industrial belt.[3]

Since that time the Coffin has remained the principal centre for multi-component manufacturing industry, but great new developments such as oil refineries, petro-chemical plants, gasification plants, and integrated steelworks have grown up outside it, attracting their own groups of industries around them. The favourite sites for these have been the estuaries around the edges of the English Plain, particularly the Severn, Solent, Mersey, Humber, and Thames, all linked with the Coffin by an increasingly comprehensive system of motorways, rail-road services, and oil and gas pipelines.

From this brief survey of the disposition of economic activity in Great Britain it can be seen that the same sorts of developments have been taking place in miniature here as have occurred on a larger scale in the Community. The Coffin and the super-core have broadly the same economic functions in relation to their respective areas, and indeed the central axial belt from London to the north-west is geographically a continuation of the Lotharingian axis, detached by the Channel from the super-core just as the North Italian Plain is detached from it by the Alps. The fact that Italy is a member of the Community while Britain is still outside it might suggest that water is a more effective barrier to contacts than are mountains, but the rôle of either must ultimately depend upon the attitudes of those on the other side of them and on the amount of physical power at their disposal.

All this is indicative of a readjustment in the economic balance in favour of the Lowland zone of the country, and it reflects a wider change in orientation from west to east. While the original motivation for this was the desirability of sites for the new industries in lowland England, the increased contacts with Europe have now given impetus to it, by increasing the significance of east coast ports and the industrial growth in their vicinities. The combination of all these things, together with the exploitation of North Sea gas and the eastward movement of deep coalmining in the East Midlands, is now producing conditions in eastern England analogous to those around Clydeside and Merseyside a century ago, with gas and oil in place of coal, and Europe taking the place of the Americas.

At the same time as the 'drift to the south', although expended demographically, is increasing the scale of southern and eastern coastal developments in Britain, there has been a 'drift to the north', in the Community, and the combination of these two is producing a high level of economic activity in a belt around the southern shores of the North Sea.

It can be seen, therefore, that the considerable increase in economic contacts between this country and the Community is paralleled by geographical adjustments which are in some ways a consequence of the reorientation of Britain's external economic relations, and in others are encouraging an increase in such contacts. The effects which membership will have on the British economy as a whole have been debated *ad nauseam* and it is not within the scope of this book to add to them.[4] It is pertinent, however, to consider the likely effects of such a move on Britain's economic geography and, as a consequence, on its regional development. This must, of course, be speculative, based on an observation of the effects which membership has had on the Six themselves. In view of the close ties which have already been built up, it is arguable that Britain is almost *de facto* in, and that formal entry would merely have the effect of making it *de jure*. However, since the full Common Market has only just come into being, it is predictable that being outside the Community for the second ten years of its existence, as we have been for the first, would certainly put the brakes on the 'Europeanization' of the British economy, so that the 'natural' development—if this is what one may call the continuation of existing trends—may only go on if Britain does become a member.

Membership of the Community will most likely accentuate the 'drift to the south' by making industrial sites in south-east England very desirable for firms exporting to the continent and having subsidiaries or component suppliers on the other side of the Channel. The sort of firms which will find this desirable will be those with a high ratio of exports to sales on the home market, those which are closely allied with companies operating on the continent and those, such as component and accessory suppliers, to whom speed of delivery is very important. In many ways sites in, say, the north-west would be just as good, but taking all factors into account the balance of advantage over a wide range of manufactures, especially multi-component and consumer goods, is with locations nearest to the major centres of European industrial development.

If British manufacturers are not to be at a disadvantage as compared with their continental rivals, the scale and variety of methods of transport across the Channel will have to be improved. In this context one naturally thinks of the Channel Tunnel and an increase in air freight, both of which will eliminate the inconvenience of the Channel. The development of hovercraft services for both passengers and freight, together with pipelines and cables for liquid and energy transfers also comes to mind. The natural line for such communications will certainly be the Straits of Dover, and this will undoubtedly result in the establishment of many industries both in Kent and Pas de Calais to take advantage of the ease of communications.[5] The development of effective links between the Coffin and the super-core can be expected to result in the emergence of an enlarged Lotharingian axis stretching from the Irish Sea to the Mediterranean, which will be followed by motorways, electrified railways, pipelines, and air services, and to cater for the increase in air traffic it is likely that new international airports will have to be constructed at its terminals in north-west England and northern Italy.

The removal of tariff barriers will also undoubtedly tend to increase the degree of specialization in British industry. Instead of producing the whole gamut of manufactured goods with the home market in mind, competition will tend to make manufacturers concentrate more on their strong lines, and industries which are not competitive in the Community market will tend to drop out. There have been many forecasts of the particular industries in which Britain's position will prove strongest, and, predictably, they are all different. However, on balance those with the greatest comparative advantage would appear to be vehicles—particularly tractors and commercial vehicles—power-generating machinery, paints and varnishes, woollen fabrics, dyes, and rubber tyres.[6] Those with the lowest comparative advantage appear to be iron and steel, cotton and synthetic fabrics, clothing, organic chemicals, and office machinery. While no clearcut geographical pattern emerges from this list, broadly speaking those industries likely to benefit most are those located in the Coffin and at estuarine sites in the south and east, and in spite of all that is being done for the old industrial regions, the disequilibrium between the Highland and Lowland zones will most likely increase. It may well be that for a large number of industries even Lowland Britain will be comparatively disadvantageous, and investment there may as a consequence be more sluggish than in the continental super-core. While retaining a high degree of resilience

146

in its typical staple industries, and possibly expanding rapidly in those industries now developing in estuarine sites such as oil-processing and petro-chemicals, it seems likely that the general rates of expansion of industry will be slower than those in the super-core.

However, in a wide range of sophisticated industries such as computers, electronic equipment, telecommunications, micro-engineering, nuclear research, aircraft, and the 'science-based' industries generally, Britain is very advanced, indeed more so than the Community, and she would therefore naturally play a considerable part in developing them for the Community market. The Community must have Britain in if it is to make any showing with America in these fields, since in the 'science-based' industries Britain is very nearly the equal of the Six put together, and, as has been said, 'a European technological policy without Britain is the blind leading the blind; Britain is at least one-eyed'.[7] At the moment she is handicapped in this field by the lack of finance and of markets on a sufficient scale to warrant manufacture, but the growth of the Community with Britain as a part of it would change all that. At the moment the principal centre for these industries is in south-east England, and it could be that Britain's head start in these things will tend to emphasize further their existing locations rather than causing them to drain off to the continent. The value of the super-core locations will, in any case, be less obvious since the lack of a suitable industrial infrastructure there would be a disadvantage, and transport of electronic components is less of a problem than in the case of heavier goods. Lowland England may, therefore, in this respect develop a relationship to the expanded Community similar to that of New England to the United States of America—as a centre of technical excellence and a producer of a wide range of sophisticated equipment. Of course, one must not press this comparison too far since the industrial development of the United States occurred entirely in the conditions of the large market, while in Europe each state has already duplicated the industrial structures of the others. It would seem more likely that Britain will retain a broad industrial structure, tending gradually to become more specialist, but that the most radical and characteristically European developments will be in the newer industries which are as yet relatively small and which still offer great opportunities for expansion.

The main point is that Britain will naturally be somewhat peripheral and cut off in relation to the new economic grouping, and as such will be very attractive only to those industries for which a peripheral location is not a disadvantage, or where there are

147

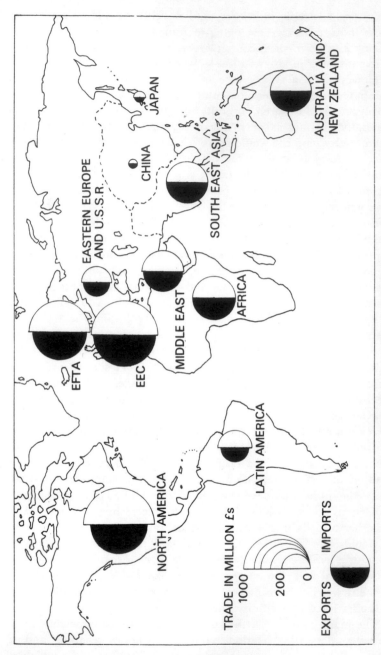

Fig. 35. International trade of Great Britain, 1965

especially advantageous local factors which outweigh this. In the absence of these an industrial site at Calais must *ipso facto* be a better one in relation to the Community market than one at Dover until communications across the Channel are such that it is of practically no significance as a barrier.

Such advantageous factors may be natural or contrived, or—in present conditions—a bit of both. In the case of southern Britain the complex and sophisticated industrial structure, large labour force, and consumer market are obvious attractions, and the relative value of these compared with those of other Community states will vary with each individual industry. From the standpoint of American investment, however, Great Britain does have the advantage of close ties with the United States, a common language, similar business practices, and an already very high American-owned sector. This country is, from these points of view, more attractive than are the Community countries, and between 1962 and 1965 $2,368 million was invested here compared to $3,557 million in the whole of the Community. Britain has been for American firms a good base from which to export goods to the continent, and sites in the south and east such as the Ford Dagenham plant and the Esso refinery at Fawley were built partly with this in mind. This is, in a sense, an economic version of the Trojan Horse idea, but if Britain does not get into the Community within a few years the increasing difficulty of penetrating its markets may cause this advantage to dwindle and divert more American investments straight to the continent.

The artificial attractions which could further modify the economic trends are those created by the government to stimulate regional growth. Ever since the 1930s successive British governments have been concerned with the plight of the older industrial regions and have labelled them 'special areas' or 'development areas', giving them the same sort of inducements to resuscitation which the Community countries have given to theirs. In 1966 large new development areas were scheduled including parts of south-west England, almost the whole of Wales, and the rest of Britain roughly north of a line from Morecambe Bay to Flamborough Head (Fig. 34). These areas have a number of permutations of physical and human disadvantages which make them in varying degrees unattractive to industry, and entry into the Community, by shifting the centre of gravity of economic operations still farther away from them, would in the normal course of things tend to accentuate these.[8] If even southern England would be to a certain extent peripheral in these circumstances, then Scotland and Wales would be doubly so, and the whole of northern and western Britain would join western France and the Mezzogiorno as problem areas on a continental scale. Joining the Community would thus give a 'cold shower' to this country geographically as well as economically, and make a strong and intelligent regional policy quite essential. Some of the present development areas would doubtless qualify for the same sort of treatment as that received already by the Mezzogiorno, but it seems likely that the Community planners would advocate a greater concentration of effort than has been usual in the British approach to regional problems up to now.

Entry would certainly result in a continued rise in the quantities of foodstuffs coming across the Channel, especially from France and Italy which have been so drastically reorganizing their agricultures with the European market in mind. In conditions of unrestricted trade this will doubtless mean direct competition between British and continental farmers, which will lead naturally to further specialization. Such things as fruit, market garden produce, and food grains may well be imported in larger quantities from those countries which have the best physical conditions for producing them most efficiently, while Britain may concentrate more on pastoral farming, both for dairying and meat, for which this country's climate is very suitable. Britain would thus become an island whose richest farmland will be largely under grass and fodder crops and possibly even exporting appreciable quantities of pastoral produce to the continent.

The effects of British membership on the Community itself would undoubtedly be substantial. It would make it a much larger unit—a population of 235 million even if Britain were the only additional member. The whole unit would become nearly 25 per cent bigger and the finance, markets, and sum of technical knowledge would also be greatly increased. As to the internal geographical arrangements, it might, ironically, tend to confirm the Rhineland crescent from the Low Countries to the Alps as the super-core since this would then be even more central than before, balanced on either side by the two great industrial regions of lowland England and the Upper Po Valley, both within an enlarged Lotharingian axis, and these might well tend to become more specialized leaving a concentration of medium-scale multi-component manufacture in the super-core itself supplied with its specialist materials and finished goods from them and from the Paris region. The continent may also be supplied with imports from large specialist terminals in Britain like those on Milford Haven, Severnside, and the Solent which could be adapted to send oil and gas by pipeline and possibly iron and coal by tunnel to the continent, thus using the excellent British harbourages to maximize the size of vessels handled and increase the speed of delivery.

The developments envisaged here are not a radical departure from those which have been occurring in recent years. However, the principal effect of entry into the Community would be to accelerate and accentuate them by creating the overall economic conditions in which they could flourish.

Table 19. Selected Figures for the Community plus Great Britain and Comparison with the United States, 1965

	Community	Community with Britain	USA
Area (Sq. km)	1·17	1·41	9·36
Population (millions)	182	237	195
Steel Output (mill. tons)	86	113	122
Total Energy Production (mill. tons coal equivalent)	324	523	1,576
Energy Consumption (mill. tons coal equivalent)	626	923	1,789
Gross National Product (1,000s mill. $)	300	399	692

(Source: Basic Statistics of the Community 1966)

Britain is one of the four insular and peninsular extensions from trunk Europe, and of them all it was only Italy which decided, for reasons already considered, to become a member of the Community in 1952. The others had developed a higher degree of isolation protected behind the barriers of the Pyrenees, the Baltic, and the English Channel, and today this continues to be reflected in the individuality of their economic structures, their policital systems, and the attitudes which their relative isolation has encouraged.

Of the three non-Community extensions, Britain is the one which is closest, both physically and economically, to the heartland of the trunk countries. Sixty years ago Sir Halford Mackinder described this unity, or partnership as he called it, when he wrote of 'a great plain, lowlying, fertile, free from long winter frosts, free from long summer drought, densely populated and traversed by slow navigable rivers which are entered by the tides. A shallow channel, tideswept, extends through the centre of that plain, so that one section of it, the plain of southern England, is superficially detached from the remainder, namely the plain of northern France, the Netherlands and north Germany. But within all its parts it presents the same conditions for the development of human societies, saving only the insularity of Britain'.[9]

Today the essential unity of this great plain is made even greater by the diminution of so many of the factors which at the beginning of this century were still combining to make Britain very insular. Its great industrial regions of London, Birmingham, Paris, Randstad, and Ruhr-Rhine are steadily increasing their contacts in business and trade and the new mobility by air, land, and sea is enabling and encouraging this to take place. Besides, Britain is the nearest of the extensions to the super-core, and in many ways its great industrial regions are northerly extensions of it, detached parts of the European axial belt.

If one can consider lowland England as part of the adjacent continent, then the Highland zone can be seen as having much in common with the Massif Central, the eastern fringes of the Federal Republic and the Mezzogiorno. Indeed in many ways it combines the problems of being peripheral with those of declining industry, and this puts central Scotland and north-east England at a disadvantage as compared with the Community's central coalfield belt. The difficulties facing the problem regions will be even greater in relation to the larger unit than in relation to the smaller, but to counterbalance this greater resources are available to the Community as a whole.

The quotations which were used to preface this chapter enshrine fundamental truths about Britain's world relations at the beginning and at the end of the oceanic period of her history. Now they are changing again, and no less dramatically than those which moved Britain from the edge to the centre of world affairs a quarter of a millenium ago, and this has in the past decade entailed a profound reappraisal of Britain's attitude towards the continent. For centuries this country has been concerned with keeping 'the balance of power' in Europe, and ensuring that no nation was able to become dominant and so muster the continent's resources to challenge Britain's maritime supremacy. Today such a great power is in the process of emerging by peaceful means and at the same time the bases of Britain's power and of her isolation have all but disappeared. The geographical logic of the situation is plain: Britain is physically a part of Europe and is getting more and more a part of it economically also. When Britain finally becomes a member of the greater

European organization it will be setting the seal to a development which has been going on for a very long time and which heralds the opening of a new chapter in the history of these islands.

The European Democratic Community—or Europe-Maghreb Democratic Community (EMDC) as it is now officially entitled—is made up of the territory formerly occupied by the six 'common market' countries, seven of the EFTA countries* and the three north African states of Morocco, Tunisia, and Algeria. Its government has powers over all aspects of the life of the superstate, although there is in practice considerable devolution of authority to the constituent units. These ceased to be the individual states in the 1980s when they were abolished and replaced by eight economic regions (Fig. 36) and these in turn are now made up of sub-regions. The boundaries of the major regions were determined by a special commission, and although in some places they are coterminous with old national boundaries, more often than not they are quite different from them. The main criterion adopted by the boundary commissioners was that the new regions should be actually or potentially viable as economic units, although in a number of cases adjustments were made on the grounds of language or nationality if local feeling proved to be strong enough. Each region deals with its own planning, industrial establishment and economic development, but since there is a common currency and unimpeded trade throughout the Community it has no say in its economic relations with the other regions. These and foreign affairs are in the hands of the Community government, which also draws up overall plans and, through the Commission for Regions, coordinates the plans which are drawn up at regional level.

The life of each region focuses on a planned core territory (P.C.T.) generally containing the main political, financial, business, and industrial centres. In some cases the old core areas dating from the

(*) Finland has joined the much looser Confederation of Eastern Europe as also have the former associates, Greece and Turkey.

national period have now been designated P.C.Ts, but for the most part they are entirely new creations on the principle of the development pole. The economy of each region has tended to

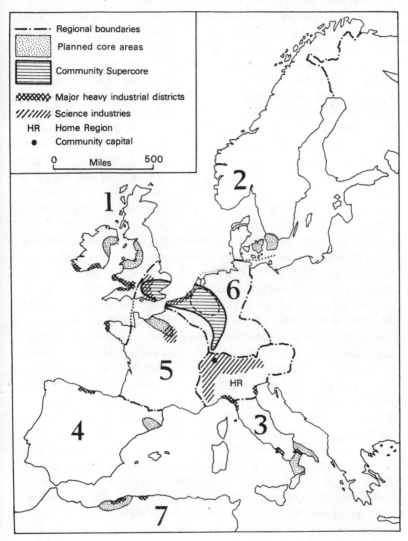

Fig. 36. Community 2000?

specialize in the production of certain goods which it exports to the others. In many cases a number of regions are still competing with one another in certain industries but there is a strong and continuing tendency to concentration. Most regions also have a great deal of general manufacture and assembly to cater mostly for their own internal needs in commodities which can be produced efficiently for relatively small markets.

Region 1 consists of Great Britain, roughly north-west of a line from the Humber to Poole Harbour, together with Ireland and Brittany. There was at first much discussion on the viability of this region, but it was decided to go ahead with it mainly because of the strength of Celtic nationalism and the strong regional feeling in northern and western England. The Irish Sea development pole, established with EIB funds proved a spectacular success, and it was designated the P.C.T. in 1987. Region 1 is also the Community's major centre of heavy industry, and has been the recipient of the so-called 'drift to the west' in iron and steel, oil refining, alloy smelting, and hovercraft construction. It is excellently located for the import of the fuels and raw materials upon which the Community so heavily depends and for moving the products rapidly to the east by pipeline and heavy monorail.

Region 2 consists of the three Scandinavian countries, and this is one of the two main producers of energy and raw materials such as wood and metals. Its core region of Zealand-Scania, like that of Region 1, was originally stimulated with Community loans, but has proved very successful, especially in the regional specialities of shipbuilding and precision engineering. Peninsular Italy, Region 3, is the Community's major producer of wine, citrus fruits, and early vegetables, and also has considerable general industrial development in the Gulf of Taranto area where the P.C.T. is situated. This was the Community's earliest development pole, and the forerunner of those established in the other regions. When Tunisia, the first Maghreb state to gain membership of the Community, joined in 1988, it was at first added to this region, but when Algeria and Morocco were admitted in 1992, Region 7, the newest of the regions, was created. With its vast area and great natural resources this is called the Community's 'new frontier' and there is now a steady movement of population across the Mediterranean to it. It has even been suggested that this 'Community California' will in another thirty years be the most powerful and important part of the Community. It now exports raw materials and power under the Mediterranean by pipeline and cable, to Marseilles and Genoa, but the local industries are increasingly requiring larger supplies for themselves. Region 4, the Iberian peninsula, is one of the great problem areas of the Community, and although it has had considerable investment, encouraged by the inducements offered by the Commission, it has not yet succeeded in attaining the growth rates and living standards to be found elsewhere. It is largely agricultural, supplying fruit and vegetables to the rest of the Community, and is also a very important tourist area for poorer families unable to afford to holiday in other continents.

Region 5 consists of France with the exception of Brittany and of parts of the east of the country. Apart from the great industrial concentrations of Paris and the Rhône corridor, it specializes mainly on intensive agriculture and is the Community's 'Mid-West' supplying it with the greater part of its home-produced food grains, temperate fruits, and pastoral produce. The Paris area is one of the only two centres of the science industries outside the Home Region, the other being South-east England.

All these six regions form a great interrupted crescent stretching from northern Scandinavia around the west of Europe to Africa, and while their P.C.T.s have a variety of industries, they specialize particularly on the production of raw materials, energy, semi-finished goods, and foodstuffs. The real industrial heart of the Community is made up of Region 6 and the 'Home Region' and here manufacturing industry is most highly developed, especially the more sophisticated manufactures which are made for the Community market as a whole and exported all over the world. Region 6 is based on the Rhine basin and South-east England. By the early 1970s the lower Rhinelands had become indisputably the Community's super-core, and, with the entry of Britain, South-east England became more and more a part of this, and its links with north-west Britain became gradually more tenuous. By the early 1980s the Ruhr-Rhine conurbation had a population of 50 million and this, together with its outlier in South-east England, and, to a lesser extent, in Northern Italy, came to dominate the Community in practically all forms of economic activity. By the late 1980s, however, its relative importance had begun to decline mainly as a result of developments elsewhere and of changes in the structure of industry. The iron and steel and other heavy industries of the Low Countries began to suffer more and more from competition from the newer ones set up on the Atlantic margins of Region 1, and the new scientific industries were widely dispersed but came to be particularly concentrated into the Home Region. In addition to this the decline in the use of road transport consequent upon the increasing use of pipelines, monorails, and private aircraft dealt a heavy blow to a staple group of industries within the super-core, and this was aggravated by the coming of a high level of market saturation in electrical and domestic appliances.

As a consequence of all this the super-core, although still the major general industrial area in the Community, now faces great problems of adjustment to the new conditions. In 1998 it was scheduled a 'special assistance' area by the Commission, and an attempt is now being made to phase the decline in its major industries with the introduction of new ones, important among which are those connected with tourism to cater for the millions of visitors who come to its great cities every year. Although they have lost a great deal of their economic and political importance, such places as London, Brussels, and Paris, are still the main cultural and social centres, and the 'pied à terre' in town is becoming increasingly popular among the Eurocrats of the Home Region. A considerable movement of population out from Region 6 has already taken place, the main inflows being westward to Region 1 and south to the 'new frontier' in the Sahara, both of which are still expanding rapidly.

The Home Region is made up essentially of the Alps together with the Po basin, and is the nerve centre of the Community. It was decided to move the various agencies of the government to this area in the 1980s and the administrative city of Charlemagne near Berne was built to receive them. However, in practice the government offices, business headquarters, financial centres, and planning departments are very widely spread throughout the territory, and the population of Charlemagne is still only 15,000 and it really comes to life only when Parliament is in session. The Home Region is also the main centre of the scientific industries and these are located all over the Alpine territories. Besides its relatively central location, its main asset is its desirability as a living area for the millions of administrators and scientists who work in it. With the efficiency and rapidity of modern means of transport and communication, this has now become one of the most important locating factors for a wide range of activities. The Upper Po industrial area supplies the Home Region with a great variety of manufactured goods, and is also the main producer of semi-finished materials and components for the use of its scientific industries.

This Community of the year 2000 has a Gross National Product and a general level of manufacturing similar to those of the United States and the Soviet Union, and considerably higher than the Eastern European Confederation or any of the other great world blocs. Until the early 1990s its deficiency in energy and raw materials was greater than that of the other two super-powers, but the accession of the Maghreb countries with their natural wealth has been rapidly decreasing the dependence on imports.

Is this a fair prediction of the sort of Europe we may be living in in thirty years from now? It is based upon an analysis of the economic and other trends which are already visible throughout Western Europe, and especially in the Community, and projecting them into the future. Such a projection can naturally only be based on the known factors, but there are always so many unforeseeable ones in economic life—a new invention or discovery, changes in social habits, and the influence of purely political elements—that it is unlikely that at a given point of time any prediction will turn out to be accurate in all particulars.

Ultimately, the thing of greatest importance is what future generations will do with the wealth which the Community can help give to this continent—whether it will be used as wealth has so often been in the past to promote limited and self-destructive aims, or whether it will be used to enrich the quality of life both for the people of this continent and for those of other continents as well.

References

Chapter 2

1 'One Community Transport Policy.' *European Community*, August/ Sept. 1965.
2 *The Sun Highway*. Italy: Documents and Notes No. 6, 1964. (Italian Information Service.)
3 M. LE LANNOU, L'Europe et le Géographe, *Sciences Humaines et l'Intégration Européenne*, Collège d'Europe.
4 'Highways to the Sun: How Community Planning Helps Extend Europe's Motorways.' *European Community*, July 1967 (Abridged version of lecture by J. N. Meyer.)
5 *Tunnelling through the Alps*. Italy: Documents and Notes No. 5, 1964. (Italian Information Service.)
6 'A New Artery for Europe.' *European Community*, September 1963.
7 G. SCHOFIELD, 'The Canalization of the Moselle.' *Geography*, April 1965.
8 'Inland Navigation.' *Italian Affairs*, March-April 1961. (Italian Information Service.)
9 R. PILKINGTON, 'Joining the Rhine and the Rhône'. *Geographical Magazine*, July 1966.
10 *Énergie 1950–65*. Office Statistique des Communautes Européennes 1966.
11 N. S. DESPICHT, *Policies for Transport in the Common Market*. Lambarde 1954.
12 P. J. KAPTEYN, *Rapport fait au nom de la Commission des Transports sur les problems concernant la politique commune des transports dans le cadre de la Communauté économique européenne*. European Parliamentary Assembly Document 106, 1962.
13 J. H. BIRD, 'Sea Ports and the European Economic Community.' *The Geographical Journal*, Vol. 133, Part 3, September 1967.
14 'Rotterdam.' *Institute of Transport Journal*, July 1965.
15 'Can Hamburg Keep Its Port?' *The Economist*, May 13 1967.
16 'Italy's New Europort' from *The Economist*, 4th March 1967.

Chapter 3

1 *Statistiques de l'Énergie 1950–65*. Office Statistique des Communautés Européennes 1966.

2 'Coal Demand Still Falling.' *European Community*, March 1966.
3 'Crisis in the Mines.' *Forward in Europe*, October 1966.
4 N. J. G. POUNDS, *The Ruhr*. Bloomington: Indiana University Press, 1952.
  N. J. G. POUNDS, 'The Ruhr.' *European Community*, October 1966.
5 *Ten Years of the Coal-Steel Common Market*. European Community Information Service 1964.
6 'New Aids for the Coal Industry.' *European Community*, January 1965.
7 *Ten Years of the Coal-Steel Common Market*. op. cit.
8 *Statistiques de l'Énergie*. op. cit.
9 *Électricité de France*. French Embassy, London 1966.
10 *The Nuclear Industry*. Information Service of the European Community, Brussels 1966.
11 'Gas from Underground.' *European Community*, July/August 1966.
12 'Community's Growing Dependence on Imported Energy.' *European Community*, November 1966.
13 *Importations dans la Communauté de Pétrole Brut et de Produits Pétroliers en Provenance des Pays Tiers en 1963, 1964 et estimations pour 1965*. Commission Européenne 1965.
14 *Énergie 1950–65*. op. cit.
15 *La Conjoncture Énergetique dans la Communauté*. Haute Autorité ECSC, Luxembourg 1967.

Chapter 4

1 N. J. G. POUNDS, *The Ruhr*. Bloomington: Indiana University Press. 1952.
2 R. HARTSHORNE, 'The Franco-German Boundary of 1871.' *World Politics*, January 1950.
3 N. J. G. POUNDS, 'Lorraine and the Ruhr'. *Economic Geography*, April 1957.
4 M. LE LANNOU, L'Europe et le Géographe. *Sciences Humaines et l'Intégration Européenne*. Collège d'Europe 1961.
5 J. H. PATTERSON, 'The Progress of the European Coal and Steel Community.' *Geography*, April 1956.
6 W. DIEBOLD, *The Schuman Plan. A study in economic co-operation 1950–9*. Council for Foreign Relations, New York 1959.
7 D. K. FLEMING, 'Coastal Steelworks in the Common Market Countries'. *Geographical Review*, January 1967.
8 D. K. FLEMING, op. cit.
9 *Finsider Brochure*. Rome 1960.
10 *Investment in the Community Coalmining and Iron and Steel Industries 1956–65*. The High Authority ECSC 1966.
11 'Steel Faces Major Crisis.' *European Community*, November 1966.
12 'Concentration in Community Steel.' *European Community*, May 1966.
13 N. J. G. POUNDS, *The Geography of Iron and Steel*. Hutchinson 1966, p. 106.
14 E. MAHLER, *L'Industrie Automobile et ses Perspectives d'Avenir dans le Nouvel Équilibre Européen et Mondial*. Lausanne 1966.
15 'The Motor Industry in Europe.' *Economist*, 9 July 1966.
16 J. A. SPORCK, 'Le Rôle Croissant des Facteurs 'Humains' dans la Localisation des Industries.' *Bulletin de la Société Belge d'Études Géographiques*, 1963, no. 1.

Chapter 5

1   *Investing in the Mezzogiorno: Why and How.* Istituto per l'Assistenza allo Sviluppo del Mezzogiorno. Rome 1966.

2   *Report on Physical Planning in the Netherlands.* Government Physical Planning Service, The Hague 1966.

3   *A New Phase in Belgian Regional Economic Policy.* Bulletin of the Krediet-bank, Brussels. December 1966.

4   *Regional Policy in the European Community.* First Memorandum by the Common Market Commission to the Council of Ministers. Community Topics No. 24, December 1966.

5   Treaty of Rome, Articles 129 and 130. The European Investment Bank, EIB Brussels 1966.

6   'The EIB's Expanding Role.' *European Community,* September 1966.

7   R. REYNAUD, 'New Trends in Industrial Redevelopment.' *European Community,* April 1965.

8   E. TOSCO, 'A European Experiment—a "Development Pole" in Southern Italy'. *European Community,* January 1966.

9   A. B. MOUNTJOY, 'Planning and Industrial Development in Apulia'. *Geography,* November 1966.

10 *Investing in the Mezzogiorno: Why and How.* op. cit.

11 M. LE LANNOU, L'Europe et le Géographe. *Sciences humaines et l'Intégration Européenne.* Collège d'Europe 1961.
    E. PISANI, *L'Europe et l'Aménagement du Territoire.* Les Cahiers de Bruges 1958 II.

12 M. BYE, 'Freer Trade and Social Welfare'. *International Labour Review,* Geneva. January 1958.

13 I. B. F. KORMOSS, L'Équilibre Régional de la Communauté Européenne. *Sciences humaines et l'Intégration Européenne,* Collège d'Europe 1961.

14 M. P. ROMUS, *Expansion Économique Régionale et Communauté Européenne.* Leyden 1958.

Chapter 6

1   S. VAN VALKENBURG, 'Land Use within the European Common Market'. *Economic Geography,* January 1959.

2   *Agriculture in the Common Market.* Community Topics No. 21, European Community Information Service.

3   S. VAN VALKENBURG, op. cit., p. 2.

4   *Basic Statistics of the Community.* Statistical Office of the European Communities 1966.

5   S. VAN VALKENBURG, 'The Evolution of the Standard of Land Use in Western Europe'. *Economic Geography,* October 1960.

6   'Farm Reform Scheme.' *European Community,* July/August 1967.

7   *Agriculture in the Common Market.* op. cit., p. 3.

8   *General Statistical Bulletin,* 1966 No. 9. Statistical Office of the European Communities.

9   *Agricultural Policy in the European Economic Community.* European Community Information Service, March 1965.

10 A. R. H. BAKER, Agricultural Policy in the European Economic Community During 1967, *Geography,* July 1968, Vol. 53, Part 3.

Chapter 7

1   M. LE LANNOU, L'Europe et le Géographe. *Sciences Humaines et l'Intégration Européenne.* Collège d'Europe 1961.
2   *Partnership in Africa: the Yaoundé Association.* Community Topics No. 26, European Community Information Service, Brussels 1966.
3   'The Meaning of Association.' *European Community,* April 1964.
4   *The European Development Fund.* European Community Information Service, Brussels 1967.
5   'EIB's Expanding Rôle.' *European Community,* September 1966.

Chapter 8

1   S. OSUSKY, *The Problem of Raw Materials and its Influence on the Fate of Europe* (English summary). Sbornil Ceskoslovenske Spelecnosti Zemepisne 43, 1937.
2   I. B. F. KORMOSS, *Les Communautés Européennes: Essai d'une Carte de Densité de Population.* Les Cahiers de Bruges 1959, II.
3   S. MANNELLA, 'Esperienze e Propositi de Integrazione Socio-Economica nell' Ambito della Communita Economica Europea'. *Rev. Geografica Italia,* Firenze 1964, No. 3.
4   'The Motor Industry in Europe.' *Economist,* 9 July 1966.
5   H. MACKINDER, 'Geographical Conditions Affecting the British Empire: The British Isles'. *Geographical Journal,* vol. 33, 1909.
6   J. A. SPORCK, 'Réflexions pour une Géographie Volontaire de la Localisation de l'Industrie en Europe Occidentale'. *Bulletin de la Société de Géographie de Lille,* 1961 No. 4.
7   M. CHISHOLM, 'The Common Market and British Manufacturing Industry and Transport'. *Journal of the Town Planning Institute,* January 1962.
8   U. KITZINGER, *The Challenge of the Common Market.* 4th edn, Blackwell 1962, Chap. 1.
9   A. LAMFALUSSY, *The United Kingdom and the Six.* Macmillan 1963.
10 H. BRUGMANS, Un Historien Regarde l'Intégration Européenne. *Sciences Humaines et l'Intégration Européenne.* Collège d'Europe 1961.

Chapter 9

1   *Britain and Europe.* DEA Progress Report. Department of Economic Affairs, June 1966.
2   'Overseas Investment in 1966.' *Board of Trade Journal,* vol. 195, no. 3722, 19 July 1968.
3   E. G. R. TAYLOR, 'Discussion of the Geographical Distribution of Industry'. *Geographical Journal,* vol. 92, July 1938.
4   'Problems of British Membership.' *European Community,* March 1966.
5   M. J. WISE, 'The Impact of a Channel Tunnel on the Planning of South-Eastern England'. *Geographical Journal,* Vol. 131, Part 2, June 1965.
6   *Britain and Europe,* Vol. 2. Confederation of British Industries 1967.

H. H. LIESNER, 'The European Common Market and British Industry'. *The Advancement of Science*, vol. 14, no. 54, September 1957.

7 'What Europe Offers.' *Economist*, 19 November 1966.

8 M. J. WISE, 'The Common Market and the Changing Geography of Europe'. *Geography*, April 1963.

9 H. J. MACKINDER, 'Geographical Conditions Affecting the British Empire: The British Isles'. *Geographical Journal*, vol. 33, 1909.

Appendix

The Road to Unity

A brief chronology of the European Communities.

1948　Convention for European Economic Co-operation signed. The birth of OEEC.

1949　First meeting of the COUNCIL OF EUROPE at Strasbourg.

1950　SCHUMAN DECLARATION proposing an international authority for the European heavy industries.

1951　TREATY OF PARIS signed by the 'Inner Six'—France, the Federal German Republic, Italy, Belgium, the Netherlands and Luxembourg. This set up the European Coal and Steel Community (ECSC) which established a 'common market' in these commodities and gave great powers over them to a High Authority in Luxembourg.

1952　A treaty was signed between the same six countries setting up an European Defence Community (EDC), but this was not ratified by the French National Assembly and never came into operation.

1955　MESSINA CONFERENCE of the Six to discuss ways of increasing the sphere of co-operation. This decided that 'the next phase in the building of an united Europe must lie in the economic field'.

1957　TREATY OF ROME between the Six establishing the European Economic Community (EEC) and the European Atomic Energy Community (Euratom). The aim of the former is to establish a 'common market' by removing all restrictions on trade among the member states and to bring about integration in all aspects of their economies. Executive power was in the hands of a Commission of eight members, subject to overall supervision by the Council of Ministers.

1959   The two Communities came into being and the first tariff cuts were made.

(On failing to reach an agreement with the Community, the 'Outer Seven'—United Kingdom, Denmark, Norway, Sweden, Switzerland, Austria, and Portugal—entered into the Stockholm Agreements which set up the European Free Trade Association (EFTA), a far less ambitious concept than the Community, concerned mainly with the removal of artifical restrictions on trade. In the following year it was joined by Finland.)

1961   Britain applied to become a member of the Communities, and this was followed by applications by the other EFTA countries with the exception of Portugal and Finland.

1962   Greece became the first associate member of the Community.

1963   Negotiations for British entry broke down.

The Yaoundé Convention was signed between the Community and 18 independent African countries all of which had been colonies of one or other of the Community countries. This gave them associate status for a five-year period from 1 June 1964 and entitled them to considerable financial aid.

1964   Turkey became an associate member of the Community.

1966   Agreement was reached on the implementation of a Common Agricultural Policy (CAP).

Nigeria became an associate member of the Community with some of the privileges granted to the 'Yaoundé 18'.

1967   The United Kingdom, Ireland, and Denmark applied for membership of the Community.

The executives of the three Communities are replaced by a single unified Commission with its headquarters at Brussels.

(Abolition of all tariffs in EFTA ahead of schedule, and 18 months before the scheduled ending of internal tariffs in the Community.)

1968   All tariffs on trade between the member states removed, and a common external tariff came into effect, thus completing the Community's customs union.

Index